CLEAR YOUR CLUTTER

WITH

FENG SHUI

CLEAR YOUR CLUTTER

WITH

FENG SHUI

REVISED AND UPDATED

KAREN KINGSTON

HARMONY

BOOKS • NEW YORK

This book is intended for educational purposes and not as a guide for the diagnosis and/or treatment of any physical or psychiatric illness. Any reader needing such guidance is advised to seek the help of a licensed healthcare professional.

Copyright © 1998, 2008, 2013 by Karen Kingston

Published in the United States by Harmony Books, an imprint of the Crown Publishing Group, a division of Penguin Random House LLC, New York.
www.crownpublishing.com

Harmony Books is a registered trademark, and the Circle colophon is a trademark of Penguin Random House LLC.

Previous editions published in Great Britain by Piatkus, an imprint of Little, Brown Book Group, London, in 1998, 2008, and 2013. An earlier edition published in the United States by Broadway Books, a division of Penguin Random House LLC, New York, in 1999.

Library of Congress Cataloging-in-Publication Data is available upon request.

ISBN 978-1-101-90658-3
eBook ISBN 978-1-101-90659-0

Printed in the United States of America

Book design by Lauren Dong
Cover design by Jenny Carrow
Title page art © by Rudyard Mace/Veer

10 9 8 7 6 5 4 3 2 1

Revised Edition

Contents

About the Author

KAREN KINGSTON is acknowledged as the world's leading authority on the feng shui art of space clearing, and a leading expert in the field of clutter clearing. Her books and workshops have changed a whole generation's approach to clutter and the energy of spaces.

First published in 1998, *Clear Your Clutter with Feng Shui* immediately became an international bestseller, establishing it as a classic in its field. It has spawned dozens of similar books, tens of thousands of articles and blogs, and a host of TV and radio programs in many countries, all addressing the issue of clearing clutter.

Karen teaches online clutter clearing courses, conducts private consultations, leads professional training programs, and is an active blogger with a worldwide following.

Born in England, she lived in Bali for twenty years until 2010. She's now happily back in England, where she lives with her Australian-born husband, Richard Sebok, who is also a clutter clearing and space clearing teacher and practitioner.

Introduction

After my first book, *Creating Sacred Space with Feng Shui,* was published in 1996, readers' responses poured in, telling me how much they enjoyed it and what great results they were getting from using the information in it. And one chapter in particular generated more letters, faxes, phone calls, and emails than any other—the one entitled "Clearing Clutter." It seems that everyone has some!

It was therefore a natural progression to write an entire book on the subject in 1998, and being mindful of the nature of the topic, my publishers and I agreed to make it a small-trim paperback so as not to increase anyone's clutter quotient too much by purchasing it.

In 2008, I completely revised the book to include many clarifications and updates, several completely new sections, and a new chapter about one of the most challenging types of clutter confronting people today—time clutter. Like the original version, the second edition was translated into many languages and sold well all over the world.

This third edition includes yet more updates and another new chapter that make the content of the book really complete. It's called "Changing Standpoint."

HAPPY CLUTTER CLEARING!
Karen Kingston

Part

1

UNDERSTANDING CLUTTER

1

Feng WHAT?

I once met a woman who set off traveling around the planet with little more in her pocket than the ticket to her first destination. But she had one extraordinary skill—the ability to read palms—and no matter where she went, she was never short of a place to sleep or food to eat. She would pick a local restaurant or hotel, meet the manager, and offer to do palm readings for guests in return for food, shelter, or a small wage. When I met her she had been doing this for three years, had already visited more than a dozen countries, and was having the time of her life.

I have found that feng shui has this same universal appeal. When people discover how much their home can affect them, for better or for worse, they are usually fascinated to learn more.

FENG SHUI

The rising popularity of feng shui has been extraordinary. I first discovered a passion for working with energy in buildings in the late 1970s, and by 1993 had developed my knowledge and skills to the level at which I was ready to teach publicly. Back then when I told people what I did for a living, their common response was a puzzled look and a "Feng WHAT?" Now they generally nod wisely, and the conversation simply glides on. Just about everyone has heard something about it these days.

Feng shui is the art of balancing and harmonizing the flow of natural energies in our surroundings to create beneficial effects in our lives. These natural energy flows were well known and understood by the ancients, and knowledge of them still exists in some cultures today.

In Bali, for example, the people still live in total harmony with both the seen physical world and the unseen energy world. Daily offerings at hundreds of thousands of household shrines throughout the land and an endless procession of indescribably beautiful and very highly evolved ceremonies in the island's twenty thousand communal temples ensure that balance and harmony are maintained. This, to me, is feng shui at its best—not just a set of principles applied to an individual building for a specific result, but a whole island of three million people in tune with the sacredness of the land and incorporating feng shui as a complete way of life. Materialism is starting to noticeably weaken the fabric of Bali's spiritual culture to the extent that it will surely not survive beyond another generation or two, but at the time of writing there is still much of this to see and experience if you visit the island.

MY APPROACH TO FENG SHUI

My own approach to feng shui is quite different from that of other practitioners because I work directly with the energy of each space. I have a highly developed ability to see, hear, smell, taste, and sense energy, so to begin a consultation the first thing I do is to go around the entire inside perimeter of the building, taking an energy reading with my hands. The history of events is recorded in the walls and furniture in the form of subtle etheric and astral imprints, and through reading and interpreting these I can detect everything of significance that has ever happened there. Traumatic or repetitive events are the most deeply embedded and have a correspondingly greater effect on present-day occupants. I am also able to find areas where the energy in the building has become stagnant and discover what needs to be done to improve its flow.

Whenever I come across clutter, its energy field is unmistakable. It presents an obstacle to the flow of energy and has an unpleasant, sticky, unclean feel to it, like moving my hands through unseen cobwebs. This is what first made me realize that clutter causes problems in people's lives. It also has a distinctive musty, pervasive odor that I can smell if I walk into someone's home, even if the clutter is hidden from sight. Actually, if I tune in, I can also smell it in a person's energy field around their body if they stand near me, because they become imbued with the smell of it. But don't worry about this if you ever meet me in person—there is so much clutter in the world that I don't tune in all the time!

The good news is that after clearing clutter, this unwholesome, stagnant energy and accompanying odor quickly disappear.

THE FENG SHUI BAGUA

One of the most interesting aspects of feng shui, and one that I will be exploring in this book, is the feng shui "bagua" grid (see chapter 8 for a simplified diagram and further information). This can be used to determine where each aspect of your life is located in any building you occupy.

For example, there is an area of your home to do with Prosperity (you can find out later in this book exactly where it is). Many people read about feng shui or attend a workshop on the subject, get very excited about it, and then rush to put it into practice without realizing they need to clear their clutter first. They hear they can hang a mirror in their Prosperity corner to attract more wealth. But what if that area is cluttered with junk? Sadly, putting a mirror where there is clutter is more likely to double their financial problems than resolve them.

This book focuses on just this one aspect of feng shui—clearing clutter—which is so vital to its successful application. It is the first book ever to explore this subject in depth in this context, and is intended as an ideal starter for those new to feng shui as well as an invaluable tool for those who have studied it for a while.

Throughout this book I refer mostly to applying the information around your home, but of course it can be used equally effectively in your workplace and any other building you occupy.

SPACE CLEARING

This is the term I coined many years ago to describe the branch of feng shui that I pioneered and have become best known for. It is the art of clearing and revitalizing energies in buildings, and is primarily what my first book, *Creating Sacred Space with Feng Shui*, was about. Since the publication of that book, space clearing has become a generic name for all kinds of energy-clearing techniques. However, the specific ceremony I developed is the only one whose effectiveness I can guarantee and is the only type of space clearing I refer to in this book.

For your life to work well, it is vital to have a good flow of life force energy or *chi* in your home and workplace. Feng shui teaches many ways to improve this energy flow, and space clearing is one of the most effective. It is a simple yet powerful ceremony to clear the stuck energies that accumulate in buildings over time and cause you to feel stuck in your life. The results are impressive, and many people choose to make it part of their regular building maintenance program so that the space is energetically as well as physically clean and clear. All buildings, no matter how well designed, benefit from having this done regularly, and feng shui always works better and faster when done in conjunction with space clearing.

In relation to clutter clearing, the three main causes of stuck energy that space clearing addresses are:

+ Physical grime
+ Astral imprints
+ Stagnant energies

Physical grime—By this I mean all types of dirt, dust, filth, and grunge. Low-level energy always accumulates around dirt; hence the old adage, "Cleanliness is next to godliness." A good cleanup is an essential part of space clearing.

Astral imprints—Everything that happens in a building is recorded in the walls, floors, furniture, and objects in the space in the form of astral imprints. They build up in layers in much the same way that grime does, except that we cannot see them, and they affect us in profound ways. For example, if you move into a home in which the previous occupants were happily married, it is likely that you, too, will find marital bliss there. On the other hand, if the previous occupants were unhappy, got divorced, got sick, went bankrupt, put on weight, or any of a million other things, those remain in the building and will generally cause history to repeat itself (known in feng shui terminology as the effect of predecessor energy). Imprints of your own experiences and anyone who shares the home with you will also form layers on top of the historical ones, causing any tough times you've had there to continue to affect you. Depending on the skill of the person doing the space clearing, some or all of these layers of imprints can be cleared to give you a fresh start.

Stagnant energies—Any kind of clutter creates an obstacle to the smooth flow of energy around a space. This in turn creates stuckness and/or confusion in the lives of the occupants. Space clearing clears the stagnant energies that accumulate around clutter, which makes it much easier to sort through and clear it.

While a space clearing ceremony can easily be done in a few hours, cleaning the physical grime and clearing the clutter can take a lot longer. In fact, it's fairly common for me to hear from readers that they glided through the early chapters of my first book, then came to the clutter chapter, and there the bookmark stayed for six months or more until they had done enough work to read on.

These are the kinds of letters I get:

> "I have now cleared out most of the clutter and am ready to do the space clearing ceremony. I feel that in the last six months I have not only sorted through every cupboard in my home but also through every part of my life. I already feel healthier and happier than I have felt in years."

"I read the clutter chapter in your book and am now on my fourteenth trash bag and still going strong. My husband is astounded because he has been nagging me for years to do this."

"When I cleared my filing cabinet I found stock certificates that are now worth $4,000! Your book certainly paid for itself."

The next chapter will start to explain more fully why most of your lovely clutter is more of a hindrance in your life than a help.

2

The Problem with Clutter

In the course of doing feng shui, space clearing, and clutter clearing consultations all over the world, I have the opportunity to visit many homes and poke about in places people would never let me go otherwise. As a result of this unusual (and sometimes dubious!) privilege, I have been able, over the years, to identify and verify the types of problems clutter causes.

CLUTTER AND FENG SHUI

It's important to realize how fundamentally intrinsic clutter clearing is to the whole practice of feng shui. Before this book was first published in 1998, other feng shui books mentioned the subject only in passing or not at all. Perhaps they assumed their readers had already dealt with this issue, but of course the truth is that most had not. Now, I'm glad to say, all feng shui books worth reading have a section on this topic and it is given the importance it deserves.

I do not consider clutter clearing to be one process and feng shui another. I have come to realize that clutter clearing is one of the most powerful, transformative aspects of feng shui there is, and in most cases, feng shui cures and enhancements are at best only minimally effective until clutter clearing has been done.

If you have already been using feng shui for years without knowing this, you will be delighted at the energy upsurge clearing your clutter will bring about. And if you are new to feng shui, you will be pleasantly surprised to realize that the first and most important steps to learning this art are already well within your reach.

CLUTTER IS STUCK ENERGY

The word "clutter" derives from the Middle English word "clotter," which means to coagulate—and that's about as stuck as you can get.

Clutter accumulates when energy stagnates, and likewise, energy stagnates when clutter accumulates. So the clutter begins as a symptom of what is happening with you in your life and then becomes part of the problem itself, because the more of it you have, the more stagnant energy it attracts to itself.

You know what it's like. You're walking down the street and you see that someone has thoughtlessly thrown an empty cigarette packet in a corner near the roadside. The next day you walk past the same spot, and the empty pack has been joined by a few more items of trash. Before long it becomes a full-blown garbage dump. Clutter accumulates in the same way in your home. It starts with a bit and then slowly, insidiously, it grows and grows—and so does the stagnant energy around it, which then has a correspondingly stagnating effect on your life.

If you somehow get your life moving again, you will instinctively want to clear the clutter out of your home and make a fresh start. It will feel like the obvious thing to do. So one approach to clearing clutter is to embark on a course of self-improvement and wait until you get to the stage where you just can't stand having clutter around you anymore. There are many self-improvement books you can read and courses you can take (and I certainly recommend that you do), but it can take a while to get inspired enough to clear your clutter by taking this route.

What I am teaching in this book is a new approach—sorting out your life by sorting out your junk, which results in a tremendous renewal of your life force energy. This is something practical and tangible you can do to actively help yourself.

STUCK ENERGY IS VERY STICKY

This is why it is easy to let your clutter stay put. You need to have some pretty good reasons to rouse yourself enough to do anything about it. That's what the next chapter's about.

3

The Effectiveness of Clutter Clearing

Every aspect of your life is anchored energetically in your living space, so clearing your clutter can completely transform your entire existence.

CLEAN UP YOUR LIFE

Back in the 1980s, I was one of the top professional rebirthers in London (rebirthing is a way of releasing inner blockages through the breath). I've always been a great one for motivating people to help themselves, and I began to suggest decluttering as extra "homework" for some of my clients who were particularly stuck in their lives. Sure enough, in the process of sorting out their belongings, they made substantial inroads into sorting out themselves. For the really stubborn cases I would tell them at the end of a session that next week I would be rebirthing them at their home, not mine. I think it was realizing the difference between how their home felt and how mine felt that shamed them into action.

One long-term client I remember was a young girl who was a recovering heroin addict. After she had had a couple of relapses, I realized I had to take a firmer approach. I refused to work with her again unless we did a session at her home and she showed her commitment to kicking her habit by getting her place fit enough for a rebirthing session. This was very difficult for her to do. Her self-esteem had sunk so low over the years that she was living in squalor. But she set to work with a will and triumphantly invited me to her apartment several weeks later. It was plain to see how much work had been done, and the change in her in those weeks was also remarkable. The next few therapy sessions marked profound breakthroughs for her.

Several years later I bumped into her in a public place and didn't recognize her. She had transformed into a radiantly beautiful woman, full of happiness and love for life, with a successful career doing what she had always dreamed of doing. She dated the change from those sessions and told me she had never touched heroin or looked back since. Through clearing out her clutter she had cleaned up her life.

YOU AND YOUR HOME

The reason clutter clearing is so effective is that while you are putting your external world in order, corresponding changes are going on internally, too. Everything around you, especially your home environment, mirrors your inner self. So by changing your home you are also changing the possibilities in your own life. Removing the obstacles to the harmonious flow of energy in your living environment creates more harmony in your life and the space for wonderful new opportunities to come to you.

GO FOR IT!

One English woman who came to one of my workshops got so inspired that she went home, called a charity shop, and said, "You're going to need to send a truck!" She cleared out all but five items of clothing from her wardrobe, and got rid of her ancient stereo system and stacks and stacks of junk. In doing this, she released huge amounts of stuck energy, which created space for something new to come in. A week later she received a check in the mail from her mother for £5,000, and she went straight out and bought herself a whole new wardrobe of wonderful clothes, a new sound system, and everything else she wanted.

She told me the check was totally unexpected, and that the last time her mother had sent her any money had been ten years earlier. I don't recommend that everyone undertake a cleanup quite so dramatically, but it certainly worked for her.

Here's another inspiring letter I received from a teacher who read my book and also went for clutter clearing in a big way:

"Five months after my mother passed, I needed something to help me get my head above water. I picked up your book . . . and was SO energized and excited. I have cleared clutter that has been stored and gathering dust for over twenty years! Bags of things have been thrown out and SO much is ready to be donated to charities. During this month of sorting, discarding and cleaning, I was given an unexpected check for $5,000, found out about an inheritance of $3,000, found gift cards and gift certificates worth over $400, found out about more income that will be coming monthly, and gathered about

$75 worth of change too. The additional income has been wonderful, but more than that, I'm energized and no longer feel overwhelmed. I'm comfortable and happy in my home. I'm reading about feng shui and applying the principles at home and in my classroom. Thank you for getting me started!"

Letters like these arrive in my mailbox every single day and are what has inspired me to actually write this book. Of course, not everyone who clears clutter can expect a financial windfall. I have chosen these stories because they show how tangible the results can be.

4

What Is Clutter Exactly?

The *Oxford English Dictionary* defines clutter as "a collection of things lying about in an untidy state." Yes, that's part of it, but it's describing clutter only at the purely physical level.

In my definition there are four categories of clutter:

- Things you do not use or love
- Things that are untidy or disorganized
- Too many things in too small a space
- Anything unfinished

Let's have a look at each of these so that you will be in no doubt as you read through this book where your own focus for clutter clearing needs to be.

THINGS YOU DO NOT USE OR LOVE

Things that are loved, used, and appreciated have strong, vibrant, joyous energies, which allow the energy in the space to flow through and around them. If you have a clear focus in your life and you surround yourself with things that have this marvelous free-flowing energy, you will have a correspondingly happy, joyous, free-flowing life. Conversely, anything neglected, forgotten, unwanted, unloved, or unused will cause the energy in your home to slow and stagnate, and then you will feel that your life is not moving.

You are energetically connected to everything you own. When your home is filled with things that you love or use well, it becomes an incredible source of support and nourishment for you. Clutter, on the other hand, drags your energy down and the longer you keep it, the more it will affect you. When you get rid of everything that has no real meaning or significance for you, you feel lighter in body, mind, and spirit.

THINGS THAT ARE UNTIDY OR DISORGANIZED

This category is for the messy people of the world and the hopelessly disorganized. Even if you keep your stuff pared down to just the things you use and love, your home will still be cluttered if they are scattered all over the place and it's difficult to find things when you want them. Probably, like most messy types, you maintain there is order in your chaos, and what's more, you need to keep items in the open to remind you of important things you have to do. But if someone actually puts you to the test and asks you where something is, at best you know only the general direction and rarely the precise location.

Everyone's life works better when they know where things are. For example, think of your bed. The energy connection between you and your bed is direct and clear. Unless you are the nomadic type, you know exactly where it is and you can connect to it in microseconds. Now think about your house keys. Do you know exactly where they are, or do you have to mentally hunt around for them? How about that bill you need to pay? Where is it? When your things get jumbled up and confused, the strands between you and them become like tangled spaghetti. This creates stress and confusion in your life rather than the peace and clarity that comes from knowing where things are.

Clutter in this category consists of things that either don't have a proper place of their own, or that do have one but have strayed from it and got mixed up with everything else. Many items seem to just appear in your life by chance, not because you made a conscious decision to acquire them. They include the mail that relentlessly arrives and dauntingly distributes itself in far-flung corners of your home, and other bits of paper that appear from nowhere and build themselves into mountainous heaps, defiantly resisting all your attempts to categorize and sort them. Then there are those impulse buys. You bring one home and say to yourself, "I'll just put it there for now"—and there it stays. Sometimes it stays there for months, years, or even decades, always looking slightly out of place and vaguely irking you in the back of your mind.

Now, I'm not advocating pristine neatness. A home that is too tidy, where everything is "just so," is energetically sterile and can be as much of a problem as a place that is a complete dump. But your home is an outward representation of what is going on inside you, so if you are messy on the outside there is a corresponding mess of some kind on the inside, too. By sorting out the outer, the inner starts slotting neatly into place.

TOO MANY THINGS IN TOO SMALL A SPACE

Sometimes the problem is simply one of space. Your life or your family has expanded but your home has stayed the same size, or it never was big enough in the first place. You can become creative with storage cabinets but the more you cram into your living space, the less room there is for energy to move and the more difficult it becomes to get anything done. With clutter of the just-too-much-for-the-amount-of-space variety, your home starts to feel as if it cannot breathe; your own breathing will actually become tighter and shallower (when was the last time you took a really deep breath and filled your lungs?) and you will feel constricted in what you can do in your life.

The only solution is to move to a bigger place or shift some of your stuff off the premises. You will be amazed at how good it feels, either way.

ANYTHING UNFINISHED

This form of clutter is harder to see and easier to ignore than the other types, but its effects are far-reaching. Anything unfinished in the physical, mental, emotional, and spiritual realms clutters your psyche.

Things not dealt with in your home reflect issues not dealt with in your life, and they are a constant drain on your energy. There are the niggling repairs such as fixing the broken drawer or repairing the faucet that keeps dripping, and the bigger jobs, such as redecorating the house, servicing the central heating or air conditioning, or taming the jungle that your garden has become. The larger the scale, the more these things impinge on your ability to get on with your life.

Buttons that need sewing on, phone calls you need to make, relationships you need to move on from—these and many other forms of loose ends in your life will hamper your progress if you do not deal with them. Your subconscious mind will suppress these things nicely if you ask it to, but it takes a lot of your energy to do so. You will be surprised at how your vitality soars if you just complete all your unfinished business.

The next chapter explores how all these types of clutter affect you in ways you may never have suspected.

5

How Clutter Affects You

Most people have no idea how much their clutter affects them. You may actually fondly believe yours to be an asset, or at least a potential asset after it has been sorted through and organized. It is only when you start clearing it out that you realize how much better you feel without it.

Clutter will affect you according to the type of person you are, how much stuff you have, where in your home you keep it, and how long you have had it.

Here are some of the main effects to watch out for.

HAVING CLUTTER CAN MAKE YOU FEEL TIRED AND LETHARGIC

Most people who have clutter say they can't find the energy to begin to clear it. They constantly feel tired. But the stagnant energy that stacks up around clutter actually causes tiredness and lethargy. Clearing it frees up the energy in your home and releases new vitality in your body. Here's what people tell me:

"I stayed up late to read your book and got so 'wired' that I couldn't sleep. Finally I got out of bed and started clearing my clutter until four in the morning! I had to go to work the next day but I didn't feel at all tired."

"At first I felt daunted by the sheer volume of my clutter but I knew I had to clear it. What amazes me is how much better I feel after each drawer, and how the energy somehow comes from nowhere to carry on and do more."

"My husband and I have both just read and reread your book on clearing clutter. I have tried for over a year to encourage him to unload some of his mental baggage and holdings. I read the book and read a few paragraphs out loud and he was ignited on fire like I have never seen. He is moving clutter out so fast and so much of it neither of us could believe it. He has so much more energy and is finally taking the time to actually finish the book!!!"

HAVING CLUTTER CAN KEEP YOU IN THE PAST

When all your available space is filled with clutter, there is no room for anything new to come into your life. Your thoughts tend to dwell in the past, and you feel bogged down with problems that have dogged you for some time. You tend to you look back rather than forward in your life, blaming the past for your current situation rather than taking responsibility for creating a better tomorrow. Clearing your clutter allows you to begin to deal with your problems and move forward. It is vital to release the past to create a better tomorrow.

HAVING CLUTTER CAN CONGEST YOUR BODY

When you have lots of clutter, the energy of your home gets congested, and so does your body. Clutterbugs generally do not get enough exercise, are often constipated, have dull, clogged complexions, and show no vitality in their eyes. People with little clutter in their lives are generally more active; they have clear, radiant skin and a twinkle in their eyes. The choice is yours.

HAVING CLUTTER CAN AFFECT YOUR BODY WEIGHT

A curious fact I have noticed over the years is that people who have lots of clutter in their homes are often overweight. I believe this is because both body fat and clutter are forms of self-protection. By building layers of fat or clutter around them, they hope to cushion themselves against the shocks of life, and particularly against emotions they have difficulty handling. It gives the feeling of being able to control things and prevent them from having too deep an effect. But this is an illusion. In Oprah Winfrey's words:

> "What I've learned through my ... ordeal with weight is that you can't really begin to work on the physical until you first get at what's holding you back emotionally. The reason we don't move forward in our lives is because of the fears that hold us back, the things that keep us from being all that we were meant to be."

I have certainly found it to be true that overweight people have many fears buried deep inside themselves, which they need to overcome in order to clear their clutter. However, many write to let me know how liberating it feels when they finally do it, and how the process of letting go of their junk also magically allows them to let go of their fat. They tell me it is a darn bit easier to focus on dieting their home than dieting their body, and when they start looking after their environment more, they naturally feel more inclined to look after themselves better, too. As one woman put it, "After you have cleared the junk out of your home, it doesn't feel quite right to keep putting junk food in your body."

HAVING CLUTTER CAN CONFUSE YOU

When you live surrounded by clutter, it is impossible to have clarity about what you are doing in your life. When you clear it, you can think more clearly and life decisions become easier. Being clear of clutter is one of the greatest aids I know to discovering and creating the life you want.

HAVING CLUTTER CAN AFFECT THE WAY PEOPLE TREAT YOU

People treat you the way you treat yourself. So if you value yourself and look after yourself, people will treat you well. If you "let yourself go" and allow the junk to mount up around you, you may attract people who mistreat you in some way because subconsciously you feel that is what you deserve.

If your home is untidy as well as cluttered, your friends may like you as a person but find it difficult to fully respect you, especially if you are always behind with everything you need to do, don't keep your promises because you are disorganized, and so on. When you sort out your home you can improve all your relationships in the process.

HAVING CLUTTER CAN MAKE YOU PROCRASTINATE

If you have a lot of clutter, you will tend to put off doing things until "tomorrow." The clutter stagnates your energy and makes it difficult to get yourself to do anything. After clutter clearing you are likely to surprise yourself (and everyone else!) by wanting to do things you have put off for a long time. People suddenly feel motivated to replant the garden, take a class, call a friend, go on a vacation, and so on. The letters I receive on just this one effect of clearing clutter are amazing!

"My husband died five years ago and I kept delaying clearing out his belongings. Your book finally gave me the courage to pack up all his clothes and take them to a charity shop, and it was as if a fresh breath of air came into my life. I know it's hard to believe at my age (I'm 71) but I have now enrolled at college to learn about computers."

"While sorting through my attic, I came across letters from some dear old friends who had moved abroad, and found tears rolling down my cheeks as I realized how much I missed them and regretted losing touch with them. To cut a long story short, I polished off the attic and caught a plane to go and see them. We had the most wonderful reunion. I am now seriously thinking of moving out there myself."

"This clutter clearing thing seems to get into your blood. Not content with clearing out every cupboard in my entire house, I am now up at dawn every morning tidying up the garden. Where will this end?"

HAVING CLUTTER CAN CAUSE DISHARMONY

Clutter is a major cause of arguments in families and between housemates, business partners, and coworkers. If you live or work knee-deep in the stuff and those around you do not, their lifestyle will not impede your progress, but yours most certainly can impede theirs. These people attracted you into their life for a reason, and you attracted them into your life for a reason. But the clutter is a low-level reason. Clear up your clutter and then you will be able to get to the higher possibilities of what you can do together, which is much more interesting than arguing about mundane junk!

HAVING CLUTTER CAN MAKE YOU FEEL ASHAMED

Perhaps you have reached the stage where your home is so cluttered or such a mess that you are ashamed to invite people over, and you positively panic if anyone turns up unannounced. Which would you prefer: to live in lonely isolation with your junk, or to have a good clear-out, repair your self-esteem, and regenerate your social life with confidence?

HAVING CLUTTER CAN PUT YOUR LIFE ON HOLD

One lovely elderly couple I met were living in a beautiful fifteen-room mansion. Their children had all grown up and left home, and they enjoyed a happy, loving marriage. The living areas and bedrooms belonging to each of their children were tidy and well maintained but over a period of time, most of their own bedroom and three of their other rooms had completely vanished under a sea of clutter. One room looked like a junk shop, with ornaments and knickknacks of every description stacked up in piles; another room was heaped waist-high with mounds of clothes; and the third room had more of their own junk and boxes of things inherited from an aunt that "needed sorting." When questioned, they admitted that they would love to travel and enjoy the last years of their lives together, but nagging away at the back of their minds all the time were these unsorted junk rooms. Whenever the question of taking a trip came up, they decided they couldn't do it until the junk had been sorted first. In effect, their shame about their clutter had kept them at home for years!

Don't let your life slip away. Sit down right now and write a list of all the things you would love to do if only your clutter were sorted, and let this be the inspiration for you to get on with it.

HAVING CLUTTER CAN DEPRESS YOU

The stagnant energy of clutter pulls you down and can make you feel depressed. In fact, I have yet to meet a depressed person who doesn't surround themselves with clutter. Feelings of hopelessness are compounded by clutter and can be relieved to some extent by clearing it, because you create space for something new to come into your life. The reason I think this works is that many types of depression are caused by a higher part of your consciousness stopping you doing what you have been doing because it is time for you to do something else.

If you are so depressed that you can't even begin to think about clearing out your clutter, at least get it off the ground (depressed people tend to stack their clutter at a low level), which will lift your energy and your spirits. It would also be a good idea to have your home checked for geopathic stress (harmful earth energies). Clutter often accumulates in geopathically stressed areas, and it may well be a causative factor in your depression. See the chapter about geopathic stress in my book, *Creating Sacred Space with Feng Shui,* for more information about this.

HAVING CLUTTER CAN CREATE EXCESS BAGGAGE

If you have a lot of clutter at home, then you will certainly want to take a lot of it with you when you travel. Clutterholics often have to pay excess baggage charges for all the things they drag on vacation with them "just in case" they need them, not to mention all the souvenirs they buy to bring back home.

They tend to create excess baggage of the emotional kind, too. Do you make mountains out of molehills, create unnecessary dramas, get upset at imagined slights? Learn to lighten up physically, and you'll discover you can lighten up emotionally, too, and enjoy your life much more.

HAVING CLUTTER CAN DULL YOUR SENSITIVITY AND ENJOYMENT OF LIFE

Just as clutter mutes the sounds and dulls the atmosphere in your home, it also mutes your ability to live life to the full. You can become a creature of habit and feel like you are living in a rut, just doing the same thing day after day, year after year. You may even become a boring person to know. Clearing the clutter allows the fresh winds of inspiration to enter your home and your life. Even moving it around your home from time to time will help to refresh the energy.

A major clear-out is absolutely essential if you truly want to have passion, joy, and happiness in your life. These feelings are the experience of vital energies flowing through your body, which cannot happen if your channels are clogged.

HAVING CLUTTER CAN CAUSE EXTRA CLEANING

It takes at least twice as long to clean a place that is cluttered with objects, and not only that, the objects themselves need cleaning. The more clutter you have, the more dust accumulates, the more the energy stagnates, and the less inclined you are to clean at all. It's a downward spiral.

Just think of all the fun things you could do in your life if you let go of your clutter and cut your cleaning time in half. And if you pay someone to clean for you, think how much money you can save.

HAVING CLUTTER CAN MAKE YOU DISORGANIZED

How often do you lose your keys, your glasses, your wallet? How many times have you searched for something, finally given up, and eventually come across it weeks or months later? Or maybe it is usually easier to go out and buy another one rather than keep looking for the one you know you have—somewhere.

Being disorganized wastes time, which is frustrating and makes you feel like a failure. Many people stay disorganized as a longstanding protest against parental discipline enforced when they were young, but to continue this all your life only sabotages you.

It is very empowering to decide to take control of your home and do what you want to do, instead of allowing unresolved issues from your childhood to run your life.

HAVING CLUTTER CAN BE A HEALTH OR FIRE HAZARD

It can come to this. When clutter starts to smell bad, attract vermin, become damp or mildewed, or begin to disintegrate in some other way, it becomes unhygienic to keep it—for you and also for your neighbors. Some types of clutter can also be a fire risk.

If you value your own health and safety, and would prefer to stay on good terms with your neighbors, clear out the clutter before it gets any worse. It certainly won't get better by itself.

HAVING CLUTTER CAN CREATE UNDESIRABLE SYMBOLOGY

What message does your clutter send out symbolically? Feng shui teaches us to be very selective about the pictures, photographs, and decorative items we have around us, which all give out a message. It is amazing to me how often people cling to objects that they say have great sentimental value and yet symbolically represent exactly what they say they no longer want.

Here are some simple examples. If you are single and looking for a new partner, dump your single items and solitary portraits, and replace them with paired objects and pictures of couples. If you are prone to arguments, don't have too much red in your decor. If you have a tendency to feel depressed, get rid of all the downward-hanging things in your home and replace them with upward-pointing objects that lift your energy.

After reading chapter 15 in this book about clutter and feng shui symbology, you may want to wipe out half your clutter in one go when you discover it is sending out the wrong frequencies for what you want in your life!

HAVING CLUTTER CAN COST YOU FINANCIALLY

What does it actually cost you to keep all your stuff? Sometimes, when all other reasoning has failed, it is the simple math that brings people to their senses about their clutter.

Let's do the figures. Go into each room of your home and estimate the percentage of space that is taken up by things you rarely or never use. Be very honest with yourself as you go through this process. If you want the blatant truth, include everything you don't absolutely love or haven't used in the last year; for a more gentle approach, extend the time period to two or three years.

In an average-size home, you may end up with a list that looks something like this:

1	Entrance foyer	5%
2	Living room	10%
3	Dining room	10%
4	Kitchen	30%
5	Bedroom 1	40%
6	Bedroom 2	25%
7	Junk room	100%
8	Bathroom	15%
9	Basement	90%
10	Attic	100%
11	Garden shed	60%
12	Garage	80%

TOTAL CLUTTER = 565%

Now divide the total by the number of areas.

565% ÷ 12 areas = average 47% junk per room!

So in this example, the cost of storing clutter works out to a staggering 47 percent of the cost of the rent or mortgage for the home. I seriously suggest you do your own calculations right now.

Perhaps you have even reached the stage where your stuff has overflowed from your home and you are paying premium rent for commercial storage space. Owners of self-storage units report booming business in recent years. In urban areas it is often necessary to book several months ahead if you want to rent secure storage space. Is this really a worthwhile use of your money? Isn't there something else you would much rather spend it on?

Your clutter habit costs you in other ways as well. There is the cost of your time to go shopping for more stuff you don't really need and then finding a place to put it when you get home. There is often the expense of buying something to store it in. We're talking here about things like storage boxes, shelving, cabinets, drawers, filing cabinets, trunks, or in more extreme cases, building a back extension to your home, erecting a garden shed, installing flooring in the attic, or constructing a second garage. Then there is the cost of cleaning it, maintaining it at the right temperature and humidity, protecting it from weather and pest damage, and transporting it when you move. You may also decide to insure your possessions and install a security system to guard them. Finally, consider the time, expense, and emotional energy it costs to get rid of your clutter when you eventually realize it's not helping you at all. Is it really worth it?

All these expenses frequently total more than the actual items themselves. Think about it. You are expending all that time, money, and effort to buy things you will never use and then paying to keep them indefinitely, for no reason!

HAVING CLUTTER CAN DISTRACT YOU FROM IMPORTANT THINGS

Do you own your stuff or does it own you? Everything you own has a call on your attention, and the more clutter you have, the more your energy is tied up in mundane matters. As the last section showed, it all needs taking care of in some way. When you clear out your clutter, you leave yourself free to put the important things in your life in perspective rather than being constantly embroiled in the details of day-to-day maintenance.

Understanding how your clutter can affect you helps you to look at it in a new way and start to make new decisions about whether you want to keep it or not. A vital part of that decision-making process also involves understanding why you accumulated the clutter in the first place, which is what the next chapter is about.

6

So Why Do People Keep Clutter?

The answer to this question is complex, and as you read through the following pages you will find that different sections resonate with you to a greater or lesser degree.

In all the many consultations I have done to help people clear their clutter, the junk itself is only the physical aspect of the problem. There are always deeper underlying reasons why clutter has accumulated. Excuses such as "I'm too busy/lazy/stressed" are all red herrings. If you make time to acquire clutter (and people easily do that), then you can also make the time to clear it. These defenses are attempts to evade the issue without looking at the psychological reasons for why it has accumulated.

Before we go any further with this, let me say first that I firmly believe that everyone is always doing the best they know how. So let's take judgment about clutter—your own and everyone else's—and dump it right now. You can also unload any guilt you may feel. If you have clutter in your life, then for some reason you have needed to create it, but now that you know better you can start to let it go. The purpose of this chapter is to help you understand why you have needed clutter in the past, which will enable you to release it and cease to accumulate it in the future. These patterns are buried deep in your subconscious mind and without you realizing it, they are running your life. After you become aware of them, they gradually lose their power over you, and soon you will even be able to look back and laugh at your previous clutter-hoarding antics.

So let's have a look at some of the reasons why you may have felt the need to keep the stuff you have.

KEEPING THINGS "JUST IN CASE"

This is the number one reason that people give for keeping clutter. "I can't throw it away," they plead, "because it is sure to come in useful some day."

By all means keep reasonable stock of the things you use regularly, but do you really need all those (fill in the blank) items you have been keeping all these years?

"Who knows?" you reply, remembering all the times you threw something out and then found you needed it after all. So let me explain why this happens and how to change it.

Keeping things "just in case" indicates a lack of trust in the future. If you worry that you will need something after you have thrown it away, then sure enough, very soon afterward, your subconscious mind will helpfully create a situation where you need that very thing, however obscure it may be. "I knew it would come in useful sometime!" you exclaim, but in fact you could have averted this need by thinking differently. You created the need yourself by believing that you would have it! If you have lots of clutter you are hanging on to because you think like this, you are sending out a frequency of not trusting, and you will always feel vulnerable and insecure about the future.

Often it is not just your own future you are concerned about providing for. You may also sincerely want to be able to help others. So then you keep absolutely everything "just in case" someone else needs it. Now you are saving things on behalf of people you may not even know yet and situations that will probably never happen. This makes it virtually impossible to throw anything away!

Some of the most poignant examples of the "this-may-come-in-useful-some-day" type of clutter I have come across are:

♦ Five aquariums kept in an attic for fifteen years by a man who didn't like fish.
♦ A whole pantry stacked full to the ceiling with empty bottles, margarine cartons, egg boxes, and the like, none of which had ever been useful in over twenty years.
♦ A large playroom full of children's toys kept for the future offspring of the couple's gay son, "just in case" he ever changed his mind and decided to marry a woman and have babies.
♦ A whole house full of possessions kept by a woman who bought herself a new home next door and didn't want to clutter it by taking all her things with her.

If you dig around in your home, you will probably find your own absurd items to add to this list.

The wonderful thing is that once you fully understand your own role in creating the sudden need for things you have finally decided to get rid of, this scenario stops happening. Instead, when you let things go, you either never need them again, or if you do, similar or better things will somehow turn up in your life at the right time. There's a certain knack to this, it's true, but anyone can learn it.

The more clarity and integrity you have in your life, the more you'll find that things come to you when you need them.

IDENTITY

Another reason you may get attached to your belongings is that you feel your identity is somehow tied up in them. You can look at a ticket stub from a performance you went to ten years ago and say, "Yes, I was there, I did that." You can look at a gift given to you by a friend and say, "Yes, I had a friend who cared enough about me to give me this." By keeping these reminders around you, you may feel more secure in who you are.

It is fine to keep some gifts and mementos of happy times, providing they still have current value for you and are not so numerous that they anchor your energy too much in the past instead of the present. You can make sure of this by having regular clear-outs to keep the things you surround yourself with up-to-date with who you are and who you wish to become.

However, clearing outdated belongings of this type can present unique difficulties. You sometimes identify with them so strongly that you feel you are throwing a part of yourself away, or if discarding a gift from a friend, that you are throwing your friend's kindness away. This accounts for the many ambivalent feelings about clearing sentimental clutter and, to a certain extent, these feelings are valid. Our possessions do become filled with our own frequencies, and the things we use often, feel fond of, or created ourselves are particularly permeated with our own energy. Gifts from friends, especially treasured items that they "want you to have," are permeated with their energy.

This, incidentally, is one of the deeper reasons why people feel so emotionally devastated when they lose everything as a result of theft, fire, or flood. They are grieving for the parts of themselves and their friends they have lost with the possessions (although with hindsight they usually come to see the event as a wonderful opportunity to have a fresh start in life).

The fact is that our own continuance and well-being do not depend on keeping certain objects in our possession. It is perfectly okay to let these things go. If you identify very strongly with certain things and want to make it easy on yourself, see that they go to a good new home. Let them go with love, and give them to someone who will appreciate and use them. In this way, you will eventually come to feel guiltier about holding on to them than letting them go, because if you hold on to them, you become the obstacle to letting those objects have a whole new lease on life with someone who will really use and value them!

STATUS

Otherwise known as "keeping up with the Joneses." This serves the function of bolstering low self-esteem. Now, I am not saying that everyone who lives in a grand mansion has low self-esteem. Far from it. But many people do create the trappings of prosperity around themselves simply to keep up appearances, and no amount of "stuff" will ever be enough until they tackle the deeper issues of self-worth.

It's so easy in our modern-day possession-oriented world to lose track of who you are and why you are here. Nowhere is this more evident than in the United States, where personal status is so often defined not by who you are, but by what you are worth. However, if you own things for this reason, you are buying into an illusion, for you cannot take any of it with you when you go. Your status as an eternal Spirit is defined by an entirely different set of principles than those set by our transient, materialistic world.

SECURITY

While it is reasonable to have a basic nesting instinct and create a home that serves your needs, there is a point where the motivation for acquiring things goes off track. Modern advertising is deliberately designed to play on our insecurities. "If you don't have one of these, you will be a lesser human being" is one of the consistent underlying messages we receive. To discover just how much you are influenced, I challenge you to try not to read the advertising billboards next time you go down the street. Unless you are in a country where you don't understand the language, this is very difficult to do. These multimillion-dollar advertising messages relentlessly condition us in very persuasive ways without our ever realizing it. We are bombarded by them—television, radio, newspapers, magazines, posters, T-shirts, the Internet, you name it—all encouraging us to buy, buy, buy.

But here's the thing—no matter how many possessions you have, you never feel secure. As soon as you get one thing, there is always something else you "need." And also, you have the added problem of worrying about losing the stuff you already have. Some of the most insecure people I know are multimillionaires. Eventually you come to realize that all things are constantly in a state of change. There is no such thing as security. It's a myth.

TERRITORIALISM

Let's look at what happens when you decide to buy something new. Suppose you are out shopping, looking for a new jacket. You find one you really like, leave it for a moment to check that there isn't one you like better, and along comes another shopper who picks up the jacket and looks interested in buying it. Panic wells up inside you—"That's MY jacket," you are thinking. And then there is the relief when the person puts it down and moves on, or the awkwardness of butting in and saying you were there first. These feelings can be very intense, but realistically it's only a jacket, which minutes before meant nothing to you.

Then you buy it and take it home, and your connection to the jacket strengthens. If the next day it gets accidentally stained, ripped, mangled by a passing elephant, or whatever, it feels like a calamity! Disaster! Heartbreak! And yet, two days earlier, before it came into your life, it meant nothing to you. What's going on?

This territorialism and desire to possess things come from a lower, grasping part of you that strives to own and control things. Your Spirit already knows you own nothing. It is a matter of realizing that your happiness does not depend on your ownership of things. They can help you in your journey but they are not the journey itself.

INHERITED CLUTTERITIS

We learn most of our behavior patterns from our parents. And if one or both of your parents are or were clutterholics, the chances are that their parents were, too, and their parents before them. These patterns are passed down through the generations.

So that you can appreciate the immensity of what you are up against if you come from a long line of clutterholics, let me relate an astonishing fact I discovered. If you go back just six hundred years in your family tree, which is about twenty generations, and if each of your clutterbug forerunners replaced themselves by producing just two offspring with their spouse, then the total number of your direct ancestors in that period will total over one million people. That's a lot of clutterholicism to contend with!

The "just in case" mentality is part of the psychological state of poverty consciousness (the opposite of prosperity consciousness), and is usually handed down from parent to child. So you, yourself, may never have gone hungry or wanted for anything in your life, but because those who brought you up once experienced such hardships, they instilled the same fears in you. Thus people in America still carry the emotional luggage of fears handed down from the time of the Great Depression of 1929, many in Ireland carry the legacy of the Great Irish Potato Famine of the 1840s, people from many nations remember the scarcity or rationing of wartime, and so on. By choosing to think differently, you can free yourself from the anxieties of those who brought you up, and when you go one step further and focus on abundance rather than lack, you will happily let go of things you no longer need. In fact, you will be eager to let them go to create more space for good things to come to you.

What will happen to your children if you don't learn how to deal with clutteritis yourself? Now is your chance to clean up your family line for all the generations yet to come, and help yourself in the process, too.

A BELIEF THAT MORE IS BETTER

Here's an example of this mind-set. In the West we have a whole se-lection of culinary knives in our kitchens. We have small knives for chopping small things and big knives for chopping big things; some have pointed blades, some are square-edged; some are lightweight, some are heavy. We carefully select the most appropriate knife for the task at hand.

Go to Bali and you will find something interesting. Not only do households have only one knife that can be used for many more pur-poses than we can imagine, but even a five-year-old child is usually more dexterous with it than most Western cooks (just ask one to peel a pineapple for you!). We have been brainwashed by advertising mo-guls into believing that we need a huge range of cutting implements, and now most of us have lost the skills to manage without them.

This "more is better" theme is constantly being touted to us by manufacturers who want to create a need in order to sell their products, and gullible folk fall for it every time. Next time one of those "useful-gadgets-you-didn't-realize-you-needed" catalogs pops into your mailbox, spend a hilarious half-hour reading it and almost getting convinced how much better your life would be if you only had a nonslip, multipurpose, easy-care whatever-it-is, and then toss the brochure gleefully in the trash without ordering. Pulling back from the brink of near-certain shopping is tremendously empower-ing, and you never would have used the gadget anyway!

"SCROOGENESS"

Entrenched clutterholics refuse to let go of their junk until they feel they have really gotten their money's worth from it. This applies even if the item was purchased at a bargain price or picked up for nothing. It feels indecent to let it go until every last drop of usefulness has been wrung out of it, even if it means that it sits on the shelf indefinitely, waiting for its time to come.

However, if you are hanging on to things for this reason, you will find that life does not treat you kindly. Good things cannot easily come into your life if you block the flow of energy by persistently clinging to outdated clutter. Relax your hold a little and see what happens.

USING CLUTTER TO SUPPRESS EMOTIONS

Do you feel uncomfortable with too much empty space around you or too much free time? Clutter conveniently fills that space and keeps you busy. But what are you avoiding? Usually it is loneliness, fear of intimacy, grief, or some other buried emotion that is easier to submerge in clutter than to cope with. However, it takes a tremendous amount of energy to keep that emotion suppressed. You will be surprised at how your life takes off when you finally face your fears and find yourself. Clearing your clutter is one of the most painless ways to do this because you can do it at your own pace.

OBSESSIVE-COMPULSIVE DISORDERS

Some people have so much clutter they have what amounts to a serious obsessive-compulsive disorder. If you have reached the stage where you never throw anything away because you are so worried you may discover later that you need it, this book will help you to understand your problem, but you will also need to seek the professional help of an experienced therapist (cognitive-behavior therapy has a good success rate). I have met people who save every cash register receipt, plastic bag, newspaper, and everything else because of the paralyzing fear of what could happen if they didn't. Then, instead of being a nurturing place from which they can launch themselves into the world, their home becomes their self-created nightmare.

While clutter clearing is by no means a substitute for appropriate therapy, it can be a vital part of the recovery process on the journey to a happier, obsession-free life. For further insights, read the story of "Mr. More, The Man Who Couldn't Throw Anything Away" in Raeann Dumont's book, *The Sky Is Falling* (see the bibliography).

7

Letting Go

The process of clearing clutter is all about letting go. Not just letting go of your belongings—that is only the end result. The most important thing is learning to let go of the fear that makes you hold on to things long after it is time to move them on their way.

"THEY'VE COME FOR THE STEREO"

In 1990, I decided I wanted to live in Bali, Indonesia, so that's what I did. Sometimes people tell me they wish their lives could be so free. They imagine that I started out with pots of money and could do whatever I wanted, but the truth is I started with nothing except an ardent desire to live in Bali and a willingness to change everything to achieve this. When people look honestly at their own lives to see what prevents them from doing something they say they really want to do, a lot of it is attachment to possessions. They have set up their lives so that they are not free to do what they really yearn to do.

Stuart Wilde has a chapter in his book *Infinite Self* called "Hold On to Nothing." In it he explains:

Everything you have is in the care of the God Force. If you come home and the stereo is missing, you can say, "Ah, they've come for the stereo," rather than getting uptight about it. It's just gone back to the God Force. Somebody else has it now. That leaves space for another stereo to come into your life. Or it leaves space for no stereo at all. Now you'll have the silence to meditate and think about who you are and what you want in this life.

And if you're looking for something to spend your money on, here's his advice:

The whole function of money is not to have it; its function is to use it. The main reason for generating money is to buy experiences. You want to get to the end of your life with zilch in the bank, and look back and say, "My God, look at this huge pile of experiences," because none of your memories are ever lost.

JUST PASSING THROUGH

Life is constantly changing. So when an object comes into your life, enjoy it, use it well, and when it is time, let it go. It is that simple. Just because you own something doesn't mean you have to keep it forever. You are just a temporary custodian of many things as they pass through your life. You can't, after all, take them with you when you die!

Everything material is merely energy in transition. You may

think you own a house or have money in the bank, but the fact is you don't even own the body you stand up in. It is on loan from the planet, and after you are done with it, it will be automatically recycled and appear in a different form without you. You are Spirit—glorious, eternal, indestructible Spirit—and your human circumstance is what can best be described as a transient "rent-a-body" situation.

Your body is the temporary temple of your Spirit. What you keep around you in the extended temple of your home needs to change as you change and grow, so that it reflects who you are. Particularly if you are engaged in any kind of self-improvement work, you need to update your environment regularly. So get in the habit of leaving a trail of discarded clutter in your wake, and start to think of it as a sign of your progression!

LET GO OF FEAR

People hold on to their clutter because they are afraid to let it go—afraid of the emotions they may experience in the process of sorting through it, afraid they will make a mistake and later regret getting rid of something, afraid they will leave themselves vulnerable, exposed, or at risk in some way. Clearing physical clutter can bring up a lot of emotions, as well, and intuitively everybody knows it.

However, the rewards of clutter clearing are well worth it. Love and fear cannot exist in the same space, so everything you are holding on to through fear is blocking you from having more love in your life; clearing it allows more love to start pouring in. Fear stops you from being who you truly are and doing what you came here to

Part

2

IDENTIFYING CLUTTER

8

Clutter and the Feng Shui Bagua

If the previous chapters didn't get you motivated to start clearing your clutter, this one is sure to make an impact.

THE BAGUA CLUTTER CHECK

The feng shui bagua is a grid that reveals how the different areas of any building you occupy are connected to specific aspects of your life.

If there is a particular area of your home or workplace that always seems to get cluttered as fast as you unclutter it, see where in the bagua it is located and check what is happening in that aspect of your life. You will likely find that this is a part of your life that needs constant attention and keeps causing problems. Our lives and the buildings we occupy are strongly connected, so it is wise to be more selective about what you keep in that area in order to bring greater ease and harmony to that part of your life.

Storing out-and-out junk anywhere can have a more serious effect. A junk room in your Prosperity area, for example, can create financial problems in your life.

An accountant who attended one of my workshops decided to

put this to the test. His business had slumped and he noticed that in the Prosperity area of his office he had a stack of broken mirrors and decorative items. He cleared them out and was astonished to receive not just one but two phone calls within a few days from inquirers who became major new clients. What was even more extraordinary was that these were large corporate businesses that had become exasperated with their existing accounting firm and suddenly decided to find a new one through the most unusual route of looking through the Yellow Pages. His accounting firm just happened to be the first name they picked. He was so impressed he came back to take another workshop and to tell us the story. I have heard of countless similar successes over the years.

USING THE BAGUA

An in-depth study of the feng shui bagua can take many years, and after reading this book you may be interested to learn more about it. However, to get you motivated to clear your clutter, I am just going to explain it in very basic terms, with a very simple diagram.

Let's say you want to apply the bagua to your home. First, get a sheet of paper and sketch the floor plan of your building—just an outline showing all the walls and doorways from a bird's-eye view will do. If you rent space in part of a house, don't draw the whole building; just draw the apartment or the room you live in.

Next, turn the sheet of paper so that the front entrance to your house, apartment, or room is at the lower edge of the plan, as if you are facing your home and about to step inside. The front entrance is the determining factor in how to position the bagua because this is how energy as well as people enter your home.

Special note for the Irish and other extra-friendly communities

Prosperity Wealth Abundance	**Fame** Reputation Illumination	**Relationships** Love Marriage
Family Elders Community	**Health** ● Unity Well-being	**Creativity** Offspring Projects
Knowledge Wisdom Self-improvement	**The Journey** Career Life Path	**Helpful Friends** Compassion Travel

The Feng Shui Bagua (simplified diagram)

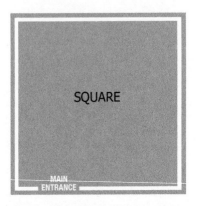

SQUARE

MAIN
ENTRANCE

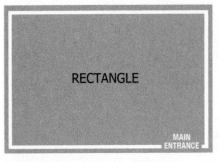

RECTANGLE

MAIN
ENTRANCE

**Examples of symmetrical buildings
or rooms**

RECTANGLE

MAIN
ENTRANCE

of the world: if you, your family, your visitors, and the postman use your back door as your front door, then use your back door for the purpose of aligning the bagua.

The next step is to draw in the bagua so that you can discover where each area of your life is located in the building.

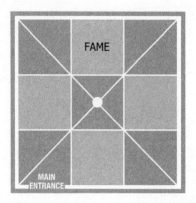

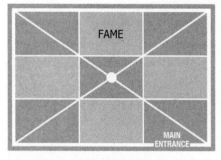

Dividing the building into the nine areas of the bagua

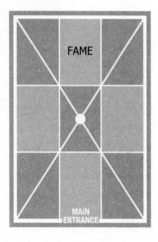

If the building is square or rectangular, this is easy. You simply divide each of the sides of the building into thirds and connect those points with horizontal and vertical lines to create nine squares or rectangles of identical size, labelled according to the bagua diagram.

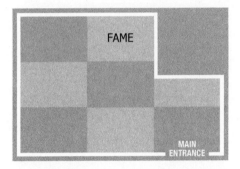

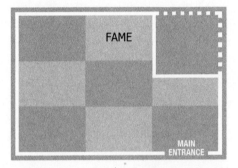

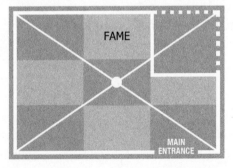

Placing the bagua for irregularly shaped buildings

MISSING AREAS

If the building is an irregular shape, you first have to square it up before you can draw in the nine boxes of the bagua, as shown in the diagrams on the previous page.

BAGUAS WITHIN BAGUAS

This is where it gets even more interesting. The bagua applies not only to the building as a whole, but also to the plot of land it stands on (swivel your drawing so that the main entrance to the plot of land is nearest the lower edge of the page) and to each room within the building (turn your drawing so that the doorway to the room is facing toward you).

So that puts to rest any ideas you may have had about secretly shifting your junk to a shed at the bottom of the garden. A junk shed in the far left-hand corner of your garden will sabotage your finances, one in the far right-hand corner will put a strain on your relationships, one in the center at the back of your garden can damage your reputation, and so on. There is nowhere you can put clutter where it will not affect you!

CLUTTER AND THE BAGUA

Try this simple exercise now. Think of a cabinet in your home that is crammed full of stuff—one that has been like this so long that you no longer know what is actually in there. That cabinet corresponds to a part of you. There is a part of yourself that you have become so out of touch with, you no longer know what is happening in there. To find out what this may be, work out where the cabinet is placed in the bagua for your home as well as the bagua for the room it is in. If it is in a room you use a lot, the bagua of that room is the most important one to look at; otherwise, just refer to the bagua of your home as a whole.

THE NINE SECTIONS OF THE BAGUA

In the following descriptions, each section of the bagua has several different names. This is to give you a feel for the different levels and energy frequencies encompassed by each of the areas. Just pick whichever terms you most resonate with.

Prosperity, Wealth, Abundance

Clutter in this area will clog up your cash flow, cause your overall financial situation to stagnate, and make it hard to create abundance in your life.

Fame, Reputation, Illumination

When this area is cluttered it can cause your reputation to dull and your popularity to wane. Enthusiasm, passion, and inspiration will also be in short supply.

Relationships, Love, Marriage

A cluttered Relationships area can cause difficulty in finding a love partner or problems in an existing relationship. What you get will not be what you want.

Family, Elders, Community

This type of clutter can cause problems with superiors, authority figures, and parents, as well as within your family or community as a whole.

Health, Unity, Well-being
Clutter here can have damaging health consequences, and your life will lack a meaningful central focus.

Creativity, Offspring, Projects
If this area is cluttered you are likely to experience blocks to your creativity, struggle in bringing projects to fruition, and have difficulties in relationships with your children or with people working for you.

Knowledge, Wisdom, Self-improvement
Clutter in this area limits your ability to learn, make wise decisions, and improve yourself.

The Journey, Career, Life Path
When you have clutter here it can seem as though life is an uphill struggle. You feel that you are in a rut not doing what you really want to do and probably not even knowing what that is.

Helpful Friends, Compassion, Travel
Clutter in this area blocks the flow of support in your life, so you can feel like you are "going it alone" a lot of the time. It also inhibits plans to travel or move your home.

THE BAGUA TEST

I'm a renowned skeptic myself and I wholeheartedly encourage you to test the validity of this information before accepting it. One way you can do this is to pick one of the areas of the bagua that is going well in your life, drag a whole pile of junk into it, leave it there for a few months, and see what happens. I did this once and it was a complete disaster!

Another, more productive way, which I definitely recommend over the first method, is to pick an area of your life that is not going well and do some clutter clearing in the relevant areas of the bagua. For example, suppose you feel generally unsupported. You would need to clear any clutter in the Helpful Friends area of your garden, if you have one, the Helpful Friends area of the bagua of your home as a whole, and the Helpful Friends areas of the main rooms you spend time in. If any of these places are inaccessible for any reason (you might have a tenant living in that part of your home, for example), you will need to do an extra good job in the areas you can get to.

Of course, the very best way to test these ideas is to clear all your clutter, wherever it is. This will help all aspects of your life equally well.

The next few chapters are about identifying specific types of clutter. Let's begin by taking a look at favorite clutter zones where junk is most likely to accumulate.

9

Clutter Zones in Your Home

Think of your home as a graphic three-dimensional representation of your own life. If you share the space with others, you may like to claim that it represents their lives more than your own, especially if they outnumber you, but you can't get out of it that easily. Everything around you is a reflection of yourself, and this includes not just your home, but any other people who live in it and what they create there.

This chapter looks at some of the primary areas where clutter collects and how this can affect you.

BASEMENTS, ATTICS, AND JUNK ROOMS

Basements

Your basement, cellar, or any other kind of under-house storage area symbolizes your past and your subconscious mind. A cluttered basement corresponds to issues from the past not dealt with, often very weighty issues (people tend to put their heaviest junk in the basement). The length of time stuff has been down there will tell you how long you have been putting off dealing with what is symbolically buried in it—and remember to add the period of time it wasn't being used before it got relegated to the basement.

If you leave things in your basement long enough, the chances are that mildew, mice, damp, fungus, or some other natural savior will intervene to help you decide to dump them. But while these processes are happening, how are they affecting your life? Feeling hopeless, depressed, lethargic, aimless, or burdened in your progress are just some of the unfortunate side effects subterranean clutter can have.

You can, of course, use your cellar for some storage, but don't have so much stuff that air and energy cannot circulate, and be sure to regularly review what is down there and keep only things you actually use from time to time.

Attics

Things stored in your attic can restrict your higher aspirations and possibilities. You stifle yourself by creating a false limitation. You will tend to worry more about the future than other people, as if there are problems hanging over you, ready to fall on you at any time. After clearing out their attics, many people write to tell me what a difference it makes:

> "It took me a week to clear out the attic but it felt fantastic and I am buzzing with energy."

> "I had over forty years' memorabilia stored in my attic—old love letters, photos, trinkets, and souvenirs. They were just gathering dust and entertaining the mice. I cleared the lot and converted my attic to an art studio,

which has now become my favorite room in the house. My new-found creativity has brought me such joy."

"I booked a consultation with you because my business had plateaued out several years ago and I was hoping you could work your feng shui wonders to move it on to bigger and better things. The last thing I expected you to recommend was to clear out the attic and I must admit I wouldn't have done it if it had been left to me. It was my wife who finally talked me into it and I just want to let you know that it has been exactly as you said—like taking the lid off my business. It has completely taken off in new and exciting ways, like a dream come true."

Junk Rooms

Hopefully the chapter on the bagua put you off ever having one of these again. The murky energy that emanates from junk rooms is highly undesirable and can really mess up whichever aspect of your life it is connected to. If your circumstances are such that you absolutely must have a junk room for a while longer, then at least tidy and organize what is in there.

Junk Drawers

What I am about to say may surprise you. My advice is: do have one. Designate one drawer that you can just throw things into. If you live in a big house, you may even need a junk drawer on every floor.

This whole clutter clearing thing is not about being obsessively perfect—it is about handling your belongings in such a way that the energy of your home is vibrant and flowing rather than dull and stagnant. In our busy world, we sometimes need the blessed relief of just opening a drawer and chucking in all those odd things that are littering the place. So do have a junk drawer but follow these three rules:

1. Choose a small drawer.
2. Use it sparingly.
3. Have regular clear-outs.

ENTRANCES, DOORWAYS, AND CORRIDORS

Main Entrance

In feng shui, the main entrance to your home represents your approach to the world as you look out, and your approach to your own life as you look in. Just as people enter and leave through this doorway, so, too, does energy. If the area is cluttered in any way it can restrict the flow of opportunities coming to you and obstruct your progress in the world. This is a very important area to keep clear. Clutter near the main entrance creates unnecessary struggle in your life.

Next time you use the front door of your home, take a long, objective look at what you see. Is the pathway to it cluttered by overhanging branches or overgrown plants? Is there junk outside the door or visible from the pathway as you approach or leave the building? Do you have to fight your way in past pegs of bulging coats hung five deep, scattered shoes, raincoats, hats, gloves, scarves, and other assorted paraphernalia? Organize this area so that it is as clutter-free as possible, and especially make sure that there is no clutter wedged behind the door, preventing it from opening fully.

Back Door

As you'll discover later in this book when I talk about the wonders of colon cleansing, everything eats and excretes. If your front door is the mouth through which things enter, then it logically follows that your back door is . . . (you can figure this out for yourself). So if you don't want your home to be constipated, don't let clutter accumulate here either.

Behind Doors

One very simple way to test whether feng shui works or not is to go through your home and clear clutter from behind all your doors. This includes items hanging from hooks and doorknobs (bathrobes, towels, bags, you name it) as well as things that obstruct doors from opening fully (furniture, laundry baskets, etc.). Then notice how much easier your life becomes. This is so simple and so effective. When your doors cannot open fully, the energy cannot flow freely around your home, so everything you do takes more effort. When you remove the clutter, the energy flows more smoothly, and so does your life.

Corridors

Clutter in corridors, passageways, and stairways obstructs the flow of life-bringing energy through your home, so your life lumbers rather than jaunts on its way. The worst type is clutter that causes you to contort your body as you walk to maneuver around it. Keep all these areas as clear as possible.

LIVING AREAS

Living Room/Family Room

This varies enormously from home to home. Some areas are kept fastidiously clean, tidy, and clutter-free so that they are always presentable when visitors call. Others look permanently like a hurricane just swept through. The important thing is that your home has a "heart" where people naturally feel drawn to spend time and hang out with one another. Even if you live alone, there still needs to be a place where you do this with yourself. A house without a heart is not a home.

Sometimes the living room or family room becomes the gathering point of this energy, or it may be the kitchen table or dining room. Wherever it is, it's important that the energy doesn't whiz through the space too quickly. It needs to be able to collect and blend before moving on its way. So this is one instance where a few well-chosen decorative objects can be placed to anchor the energy and create a homey atmosphere. Make this space as inviting as possible; it is particularly important to have an attractive centerpiece that symbolizes something relevant and inspiring to the people who live there. But if you have too much clutter, the heart of your home will become stagnant, so it's important to get the balance right.

Kitchen

What is lurking in your kitchen cabinets? A man who came to one of my workshops shared with the group that after reading my book he decided to eat his way through all the food he had and not go shopping again until he had consumed the lot. He said he managed to live like this for nearly eight weeks. In the end he was down to ten cans of food he didn't like, so he threw them out and went shopping!

Have a major clear-out of all your cabinets, as well as your fridge and freezer.

BEDROOMS

Things That Don't Belong in Bedrooms

Is your bedroom a dumping ground for all those things you have nowhere else to put? If so, you are treating yourself like a second-class citizen. It's really not ideal to have computers, exercise bikes, broken-down equipment, and other unseemly objects crowded into your sleeping area. Clutter in the bedroom is a real no-no, for children and adults alike.

For those who are romantically inclined, whether you are single and looking or already in a relationship, keeping your bedroom tidy and clutter-free will pay dividends. Stale energy hangs around dirty laundry, so never keep a laundry basket in the bedroom, and be sure to change your sheets at least once a week to keep your energy fresh and vital. These tips will improve the quality of your sleep as well as your love life.

Under Beds

Anything in your energy field affects the quality of your sleep, so resist the temptation to stash junk under your bed. If you have one of those beds with drawers underneath, the best things to keep in there are clean bed linens, towels, or clothing.

Tops of Dressers

It is a curious and little-known fact that when people have lots of bottles and containers on their dressers, most of them are almost empty. Check yours and see!

Keep the surfaces in your bedroom as clear as you can so that the energy can move smoothly and harmoniously around the space.

Tops of Closets

Clutter crammed on tops of closets is like problems hanging over you waiting to be dealt with. It impedes your ability to think clearly and freshly, and if it's the first thing you see when you wake up in the morning, you will tend to feel sluggish. Lots of clutter in your home stashed higher than eye level has a generally oppressive effect, and you may suffer from headaches.

Inside Closets

Most people wear about 20 percent of their clothes 80 percent of the time. If you doubt me, do this test for a month: each time you wear something and launder it, hang it at one end of your closet.

At the end of the month you will find (unless you have deliberately changed your habits to beat this exercise or have a job that requires you to vary your outfits often) that you are wearing these same clothes most of the time.

Actually it's not just the clothes you wear that follow this 80/20 pattern. It can be applied to everything else you own and to most activities in life. We all get 80 percent of our results from 20 percent of our efforts (this is known in the business world as the Pareto principle, named after an Italian economist who first figured it out). Similarly, we get 80 percent usage from 20 percent of our belongings.

So when it comes to clearing out your wardrobe, first separate your clothes honestly into the 20 percent you love to wear and the 80 percent that are just taking up space. Then it becomes much easier to dump the excess.

When sorting through your 80 percent pile, it is wise to get clear on your criteria for whether something stays or goes. First check out the colors. A great investment is to have a professional color consultation and discover which colors uplift and enhance your energy and which ones do the opposite. You will walk away with a swatch of color samples that are sure to make you look and feel great, which does wonders for your self-esteem. This helps you to sift through and discard at least 50 percent of these clothes because it suddenly becomes abundantly obvious that they never did anything for you in the first place.

Next, try on each item in the remaining pile and see how you feel. If you don't like the shape, texture, cut, material, or anything else about it, let it go. You owe it to yourself to create a collection of outfits you absolutely love, so that never again do you open a closet bulging with clothes and moan, "But I've got nothing to wear!"

Make a decision to never, ever buy anything again that isn't quite what you want, because now you know it will just end up in the 80 percent pile, and you will have wasted your money. Resolve to buy only clothes that you love and that look great on you, and if this means that you buy three great outfits that cost a little more rather than ten cheaper ones you'll never enjoy wearing, so be it. And yes, I recommend you do this even if you are short of money. In fact, making a point of always looking good and feeling good is one of the best ways to raise your energy and thereby attract prosperity.

Some people keep things they haven't worn in over twenty years. They say that if they keep them long enough they will come back into fashion. My advice is: if you haven't worn it in the last year, and especially if you haven't worn it in the last two or three years, then fling it, sell it, exchange it, or give it away. In one year you will have cycled through all the seasons, and if you haven't felt the urge to wear it in all that time, then that particular article of clothing has had its day. If two or three years have gone by without you wearing it, then it is definitely time to let it go.

It may be useful to understand why these clothes will never be appropriate again. In the same way that we decorate the walls of our homes, we choose clothes whose colors, textures, and designs reflect our own energy vibrations. As an example, people go through color phases. There was a time, years ago, when almost my entire wardrobe was purple. I had a few green, blue, and turquoise items, but it was purple I was really big on. Someone came to find me in Bali and knew which house was mine by the sheer quantity of purple laundry hanging out to dry! At that time, I was cultivating purple in my energy, which had to do with reclaiming my own power and developing prosperity. Now I have integrated the color, so I hardly ever wear it.

Most people have some items in their wardrobe that they bought, wore once, and never wore again. What happens is that you're out shopping one day and your eye catches something—let's say it's orange with purple polka dots. You try it on and it looks fantastic (to you), so you buy it. Well, it so happened that on that particular day you were a bit off-balance emotionally, and the colors in your energy field had changed to orange with splotchy purple bits, or something complementary to those colors, so the new clothes looked great. But by the next day that particular emotional set has dissipated, your energy field is back to its usual colors, and the item doesn't look so great to you anymore (it never did to anyone else). You wait for the cycle to come around again but usually (mercifully) it's a one-time event with few or no repeats. The trick is: never go shopping when you feel emotionally out-of-sorts. Comfort shopping is one sure way to end up with a wardrobe of clothes you will never wear.

Some people hang on to clothes that are too small for them because they plan to lose weight so they can wear them again. It rarely happens this way. Throw all these clothes away, and go out and buy yourself something that makes you look and feel really good exactly as you are now. And guess what usually happens? You lose weight. And the reason is that you have stopped resisting being fat. You have decided to love yourself exactly as you are instead of waiting until you lose weight. What you resist persists, and when you stop resisting, it stops persisting!

BATHROOMS

Some bathrooms are stacked to the hilt with appliances and beauty and grooming products—on shelves and window sills, on top of the toilet tank, around the bathtub, next to the sink, on the floor, and anywhere else there is space. This makes it much more difficult to clean all the inevitable grungy deposits they leave, and creates a confused, chaotic theme in an area that ideally needs to be calm and peaceful. People with clutter-free bathrooms find that some of their best ideas (and also their best songs!) happen in the bathtub or shower. For best results, install some storage cabinets and keep them organized and clean, inside and out.

GARAGES AND CARPORTS

A clutterholic's delight! A great place to store parts of cars you no longer own, bits of furniture you no longer use, boxes of stuff you never did like, and everything else you can't squeeze into the house. The dedicated pack rat will gladly leave his or her expensive car parked outside in all weathers while worthless clutter is kept in the garage safe and dry. I even know families who have moved from a house with a single attached garage to one with a double attached garage, simply because they needed the extra clutter storage space!

Garages can be used to store things, but only items you use and like. A clean, well-organized garage space can be very satisfying.

Cars

The state of most people's cars is a real giveaway as to their true state of clutterdom. If you have cleared the clutter in your home but are driving around knee-deep in rubble, there's still work to do.

Your car is like a small world unto itself. Do you cringe and apologize for the state of it whenever you give someone a lift? How many times a week do you think to yourself, "This car really could do with a good clear-out." Every time you think about it, your energy dips, until eventually it is costing you more energy not to clean it than to just roll up your sleeves and get on with it. You know how good it feels when the car has been freshly tidied and vacuumed. Treat yourself!

PORTABLE CLUTTER

I'm talking here about handbags, wallets, briefcases, trouser pockets, and so on. Now just in case you wonder if I walk my talk or just write books advising other people what to do, here's a story about something that happened when I was writing the original text of this book. I went to visit some friends, and their two-year-old child decided it was guest-handbag inspection time. Out it all came, piece by piece, while her mother and father looked fondly on. Apparently this little girl ransacked handbags regularly, leaving a trail of embarrassed women in her wake.

I can assure you it is a wonderful feeling to sit back and watch with enjoyment rather than concern. Her parents had been prepared to apologize to me, but instead they awarded me the prize for the tidiest handbag they had ever seen.

Of course, it's not always so immaculate, but I really can't see the point of carrying a bag of litter with me everywhere I go, so regular clear-outs are as fundamental to me as laundering my clothes.

ON AN INTERNATIONAL NOTE

I've noticed that clutter zones vary from country to country. In Australia, for example, people usually have garages or storage areas under the house, so this is where they tend to put their clutter. In England, attics and basements are a favorite. In Ireland, they love to fill sheds and outbuildings behind the house. And Americans just stash stuff EVERYWHERE!

10

Collections

Most people collect something. The less imaginative go for thimbles, teaspoons, matchboxes, business cards, coasters, and stamps, while the more eccentric gather deceased pop star memorabilia, antique exhaust pipes, sewing machine attachments, even cats' whiskers (yes, I've actually met people who collect such things).

Another favorite is decorative objects in the form of animals. These have global popularity. Most sought after are cats, dogs, frogs, and ducks, with local variations such as kangaroos and koalas Down Under; elephants, tigers, and dragons for the more Orientally inclined; and so on.

Having a few cute kittens on the mantelpiece is one thing, but these collections get out of control. Soon there are cat decorations in every room, cat pictures on every wall, cats on your dish towels, place mats, teacups, and T-shirts. I was talking about this subject once at one of my workshops in Ireland. After a while, a woman sitting in the front row could no longer contain herself and burst out with the public confession that she had over two thousand frog decorations in her home. "Even my front door is made of a huge carved frog!" she exclaimed, with such pathos that she reduced the audience to hysterical laughter.

So why do people collect things? If they trace it back, some people find that their attraction to what they have chosen to collect began during childhood. For others, it was a gift they received that well-meaning friends and relatives then added to. Whatever the case, when we feel moved to collect a particular type of thing, or even when we "accidentally" end up with such a collection, what we are in fact doing is responding to an intuitive yearning to gather a particular type of essence that is important for our own personal growth. It's a specific frequency that we need to bring into ourselves at that time, and this is entirely valid. But life is constantly changing and moving, and it's actually only necessary to collect that essence for as long as it takes to spiritually integrate it into our life. Then we can move our focus to something new.

The Native Americans knew a great deal about animal essences. Each person was known to have an animal totem, which was both a protection and a source of power and wisdom. Members of the tribe would often take names such as "White Eagle," "Dancing Bear," and so on, and they would have an affinity to that essence throughout their lives.

But times have changed. In the olden days in England they would call a man "Jack the Smith" or "John the Fisher" after his trade (which became shortened to Jack Smith and John Fisher). The speed at which we live has now increased so much that the modern equivalent would be something like "Richard the Computer Programmer Turned Taxi Driver Turned Organic Farmer Turned Author." Most people can expect to have several professions in their lifetime, and probably several marriages or primary relationships, too. It is as if we are now living many lifetimes in the space of one.

The reason for this lies in the unseen worlds of energy. We are living in a time when higher levels of human development are open to us than ever before. Therefore, the last thing we want to do is get stuck on collecting frogs when there is a whole world of exciting new possibilities out there just waiting to be tapped.

THE MAN WHO MADE PIGS

One man I knew got into making pigs. It all began when his mother bought a plaster pig in a junk shop, and he liked it so much he made a mold and copied it. Soon he progressed from plaster pigs to painted porcelain pigs. Then someone suggested he put wings on them to make them look more interesting, and thus the flying pig was born. He opened a kitsch market stall in London's fashionable Covent Garden and sold flying pigs by the thousand. He made them in different sizes, and people bought them in sets to hang on their walls. At Christmas he made special heaps of sleeping pigs.

Looking back, he says he had always felt from the start that there was a purpose, some reason why he felt compelled to make them, but it took sixteen years for him to discover what that was and for his passion for pigs to be played out. He found out that his mother's father and both his mother's grandfathers had all been— pork butchers! He estimates that his final total of over thirty-two thousand pigs roughly equaled the number of pigs his ancestors may have slaughtered in their lifetimes. The karmic debt rebalanced, he closed his stall and moved on to a new life as a shiatsu massage therapist!

THE DUCK WOMAN

In the house of one woman for whom I did a feng shui consultation, I counted over a hundred ducks as she showed me around.

"What's with the ducks?" I asked her, only to be met with a blank stare. "What ducks?" she asked. We went around again and when I pointed them all out to her, she was astonished. They were in her wallpaper, embroidered on her cushions, decorating her bathroom, on the front of her nightgown, on her tableware. It was total duck-dom, but she was completely unaware there were so many. What was even more revealing was that every duck was a solitary one, and the big issue in her life was that she had never married.

To cut a long story short, she took my advice, dumped her ducks, and found her man!

DON'T BE A "HECTOR THE COLLECTOR"

The art of understanding collections is to find out why you are collecting, learn from it, and then move on. Don't limit yourself. Make space for something new to come into your life. Don't be a "Hector the Collector" all your life without ever realizing why.

If it's decorative objects of the animal kind you find yourself collecting, a good way to discover why you are so attracted to your chosen beast is to research it. Find out all about its characteristics, behavioral peculiarities, special talents, and so on. This will give you insights into the qualities you are unconsciously wanting to draw to yourself.

It may take awhile for you to integrate this information to the point where you feel ready to let go of your collection and move on, and even then, dumping all your ducks may seem too much to handle in one go. It is very important to let this process happen naturally rather than forcing it, so just gradually trim your flock as you feel able.

11

Paper Clutter

What is it about paper that is so attractive? It was predicted that the electronic age would reduce the amount of paper produced, but we use more of it now than ever. This, of course, is because attached to every computer is . . . you guessed it . . . a printer!

Here's how to deal with some of the most challenging types of paper clutter.

BOOKS

Holding on to old books is a very common problem, especially for people with inquiring minds. To many, their books are like faithful companions. They are always there to keep you company, to impart knowledge, inspire, entertain, and stimulate in a myriad of different ways.

But the problem with holding on to old books is that it doesn't allow you to create space for new ideas and ways of thinking to come into your life. Your books symbolically represent your ideas and beliefs, and when you have too many of them filling bookshelves in your home, you become set in your ways and develop fusty energy like the fusty old books you surround yourself with.

Often when I am called in to do a consultation for an educated person who is having difficulty finding a love partner, I find that in the Relationships corner of the house, or the Relationships corner of a much-used room, there is a large bookcase stuffed full of books. They place it there without knowing anything about feng shui because it "feels right" there—because in fact their primary relationship is with their books! These are the type of people who also have a pile of books by the bed for nighttime reading—again, a relationship substitute. By moving the bookcase or at least clearing some space in the bookshelves, they create room for new interests and relationships in their life.

Maybe you have so many books that they have long outgrown your bookshelves and taken up residence in other locations. Are they stacked high on your desk, on the coffee table, next to your favorite armchair, or in the bathroom? (See chapter 20 for the deeper implications of this habit.)

Learn to let your books go when it's time. Begin with cookbooks you've never used (no, don't open them to check for recipes!). Move on to textbooks and reference books you haven't touched in years, children's books you or your children have outgrown, novels you weren't interested enough to begin or finish, books with theories you don't agree with. Progress to volumes that are in such inaccessible places you haven't touched them in decades or are so old they have disintegrated with age. Then there are books that inspired you deeply years ago but whose concepts are now so much a part of you, you no longer need to read them.

Aim to end up with a collection of books that represent you as you are today and the intended "you" of tomorrow. If you're a person with serious intellectual pursuits, this may amount to a substantial library that a part of your consciousness rests on and engages with.

For most people it will just be a bookcase or two. Keep some reference books that you commonly use, allow yourself the luxury of a few other books simply because you love them or love your associations with them, and let the rest go.

Donating books to your local library is an excellent solution if you are really anxious that you will miss them. It is very comforting to know that if you ever need them, you can borrow them back for a while. In the meantime they are being useful to others instead of clogging up your bookshelves and clogging up your life. The interesting thing about donating books to the local library is that people very rarely find they want to borrow them back. After letting them go, they move on to something new in their lives and forget all about those old tomes.

MAGAZINES, NEWSPAPERS, AND CLIPPINGS

In one house I visited there was a whole room full of airplane magazines that had been waiting over twenty years to be sorted so that the owner could discover which issues he was missing to complete the set. When I asked him what he would do when the collection was complete, he was dumbfounded. He had to think for a long time to remember why he wanted them. Collecting had become the goal, rather than using them for any purpose. When he gave himself permission to stop collecting and just let them go, he wrote to tell me what a huge relief it had been to take them to the local recycling center, and how wonderful it was to have an extra room in his house so that he could now invite guests to visit!

The study of another client had vanished under a sea of newspapers and magazines she was keeping until she had time to sort through them for articles. There were also three enormous piles of clippings next to her desk, awaiting further sorting and filing. When I suggested she could dump the lot and give herself a fresh start, there was a look of panic in her eyes, as if this could have life-threatening consequences! When we took a minute to look at this objectively together, it came down to her being genuinely afraid that she would inadvertently throw away some article that would prove to be vital to her existence. This is a variation on the "this-may-come-in-useful-one-day" syndrome, which is based in fear rather than in trusting life to bring you exactly what you need when you need it.

It is wonderful to want to keep learning all the days of your life. But we are bombarded today by so much information (see "Handling Information Overload" in chapter 21) that we need to be selective. If you want to keep clippings, create a filing system for them and keep it up-to-date. Sort them periodically and get rid of information that is no longer current. If you have a pile of clippings waiting to be filed, set yourself a reasonable time period (say, by the end of the month), and if they ain't filed by then, file 'em in the recycling bin. When you have finished with your magazines, don't hog them. Pass them on to hospitals, dentists, nursing homes, schools, and other public places where they can be used; give them to relatives, friends, or colleagues who will enjoy them; or just recycle them. But move them on.

I encouraged this woman to sit down and make a list of the many things she wanted to do in her life that she wasn't allowing herself to do because of unfinished jobs such as this. This gave her a completely new perspective from which to review all the tasks she had set for herself, and it became an easy decision for her to keep just one recent pile of magazines and send the rest on their way. The next time I saw her, the change was remarkable. The grayish gloom that had hung around her had disappeared, even the bags under her eyes had all but vanished, and everything about her had become animated and alive. It seemed she had not stopped with newspaper clippings but had cleared her entire study of clutter, and then her entire house. She had totally revitalized her life.

SENTIMENTAL STUFF

This category of clutter includes wedding memorabilia, Christmas and birthday cards from years gone by, postcards, personal diaries from way back when, your children's crayon masterpieces, and so on. The older you get, the more you have. You rarely look through any of it, but you like to know it is there.

My advice? Keep the best and fling the rest! Keep the things you really love, that have wonderful, fond associations. Let go of any items you are keeping out of a sense of guilt or obligation, have ambivalent feelings about, or just have too many of. Open the door to happy new experiences in your life rather than dwelling in the past.

One woman I met had drawers and drawers full of Christmas and birthday cards that had been sent to her, which she assured me had such sentimental value she could never part with them. But when we sat down and looked through them together, she became sadder and sadder, grieving for the happiness of times gone by. Making the decision to clear them out and start to build her social life afresh marked the beginning of her transformation from the lonely individual she had become to the socially outgoing person she longed to be.

If you have huge quantities of sentimental objects, the first pass is unlikely to be enough. You will probably need to refine the process even further by going through them again at a later date. It will be an ongoing process that may seem hard at first, but it does get easier every time you do it.

PHOTOS

Do you have drawers or albums stuffed full of photos? Enjoy your photos while they are current. Make colorful montages, put them on the wall, stick them on your notebooks, make postcards, and send them to your friends. Really get the most from them while their energy is fresh and new. Don't keep photos that remind you of tough times in the past. Just keep the ones that make you feel good and let the rest go. Clear the space for something new and better in your life.

These days, many people don't even print their photos. If you have a digital camera and store your images electronically, they take up no physical room at all. Energetically this is a huge improvement, but if this now means you have excessive quantities of disorganized images on the hard drive of your computer, you have a different problem to deal with. You'll need software to help you catalog them, and then spend hours of your life doing so. It takes only a click of a button to take a photo, but a heck of a lot longer to index them so you can find them again when you want to.

If you're a compulsive photo-snapper, discover why you do this. You may well be generating the type of clutter described in chapter 6 as "identity" clutter if you take photos so you can look at them years later and say to yourself, "I was there, I did that." But if you did nothing useful while you were there, what is the point of cataloging it? It could just as easily be the case that you sit down at the end of your life, look through all your photos with a wiser eye, and ask yourself, "What was the point of going to all those places? I was too busy taking photos to really experience them and learn from being there!"

CLEAR YOUR DESK

If you have a desk at home or at work, this section is for you. The first step is to do one simple sum: calculate the percentage of naked desk you can actually see. Don't cheat and tidy your desk before you do this. Just leave it exactly as it is to get an honest appraisal of your situation.

Now, I've seen hundreds of desks in my consultancy work, in both businesses and private homes, and one thing most of them have in common is that there is virtually no space where a person can work. Usually an area about the size of a piece of paper has been left free and everything else is occupied, either with equipment or with stacks of paper waiting for attention.

My advice: *Clear Your Desk*! There was once a wonderful book by Declan Treacy with just that title (sadly, it's no longer in print), in which he described the desks and business practices of some of the top entrepreneurial businesspeople in the world, who all keep paperwork to a minimum. A clear desk means a clear mind, and a clear mind has vision and perspective. If you are bogged down in paperwork, that's exactly where you'll stay.

Working with a clear desk increases productivity, creativity, and job satisfaction. An excellent habit to acquire is to always leave your desk clear whenever you finish. It is psychologically far more uplifting to start with a clear desk than with mounds of paperwork, which makes you feel defeated before you even begin.

So start now by removing from your desk absolutely all paperwork that awaits your attention and all objects that are not absolutely vital. I'm talking here about leaving only real essentials, such as a computer, telephone, pen, and notebook. Keep other extraneous equipment such as staplers, pens, paper clips, fluffy toys, and bags of munchies on a nearby shelf or in your desk drawer.

TAKING CONTROL OF YOUR PAPERWORK

Here are some tips to help you tame your personal paper tiger:

- Get into the habit of ruthlessly reducing superfluous paperwork as much as you can.
- Never jot down messages to yourself on loose pieces of paper. Keep them all in one book and periodically transfer important information to your filing system or computer.
- Use your bulletin boards only for things that are current. If you want to remind yourself to do something, put it on your calendar. Sticky notes clutter your mind and make you more likely to forget to do things. Lots of reminder notes dissipate your energy.
- Bring your financial paperwork up-to-date and keep it that way. You are far more likely to create prosperity in your life if you become more conscious about dealing with this aspect. Create systems for paying bills on time, file things where you can find them, and love the fact that every bill you receive means you are still credit worthy! When you learn to pay what you owe with as much joy as receiving what you're due, you will have discovered how to enjoy this money game we humans have created for ourselves, rather than get stressed by it.

VIRTUAL CLUTTER

Virtual clutter on your computer can be just as much of a problem as the more tangible variety if you have limited storage capacity. Rather than waiting until your hard drive is full to start paring down documents you no longer need, a better way is to do a little every day. Go through your data files and delete old documents or transfer them to an archive system of some kind. Reorganize your filing system within your computer if necessary.

However, with data storage systems costing less and increasing exponentially in size with every passing year, this isn't so necessary. My advice is to invest in a storage system that has all the capacity you require, and then develop your search engine skills so that you can find things when you need them. You'll be happy to know that virtual clutter does not create the same kind of stagnant effect in your life as physical clutter, so providing you have computer skills and enough storage capacity, your hard drive is really only cluttered if you can't instantly navigate your way around it. Invest some time in creating a filing and retrieval system that works and you can keep as many files as you want.

TAKING CONTROL OF YOUR EMAIL

With email addiction affecting a significant percentage of the population, here are two essential pieces of advice about how to tame it and prevent it from cluttering your workday:

- Turn off any alert that tells you an email has just arrived in your inbox. The section about interruptions in chapter 17 explains why this is so important.

◆ Never check your email first thing in the morning. I mean it. Unless your job relies on checking messages, they can be a huge distraction, leaving you at the end of the day feeling like you've dealt with them all, but achieved little else. I find my mornings are so productive and valuable that I don't check email until I've completed the major task I've set for myself that day, which usually means not until the afternoon.

12

Miscellaneous Clutter

Clutter comes in all shapes and sizes. Here are some common items found lurking in many a home.

THINGS YOU NO LONGER USE

This is clutter created when life moves on and your belongings don't. It includes:

- Outdated leisure equipment (games no one ever liked, sports no one plays anymore, hobbies you have no interest in now, toys your children have long since outgrown, and so on)
- Audio equipment you'll never use again (such as speakers to a sound system you no longer own, amplifiers that hiss and growl)
- Fitness equipment you conscientiously purchased and never used after the initial inspiration wore off (apparatuses for tummy-flattening, thigh-trimming, muscle-building, and so on)

- Health and beauty equipment that's had its day (hair stylers, foot massagers)
- Gadgets purchased to make life easier that proved too much trouble to use
- Aging garden equipment (rusting lawnmowers, scruffy garden furniture, statues with missing limbs)
- Car accessories you no longer use (roof racks, tires, assorted spare parts)

And on and on. I can't even begin to cover the list of strange and curious items people have around their properties that they haven't used in ages and will never use again. You can have a good chuckle to yourself as you come across some of your own.

If you have particularly fond attachments to things you no longer use that date back to your tender childhood years, here's something you can do that many people find very satisfactory and liberating: photograph them for posterity and then let them go. The photos will retain those heartwarming memories forever and can be stored in a fraction of the space the items themselves take up. Or better still, store them digitally on your computer in a "happy memories" folder.

UNWANTED GIFTS

This can be a very sensitive issue for some people. However, here's my very best advice on what to do with unwanted gifts: GET RID OF THEM.

Here's why. Things you really love have a strong, vibrant energy field around them, whereas unwanted items impart uneasy, conflicting energies that drain rather than energize you. They actually create an energetic gloom in your home.

The very thought of letting them go is horrifying to some people. "But what about when Aunt Jane comes to visit and that expensive item she gave us isn't on the table?" Whose table is it anyway? If you love the item, fine, but if you keep it in your home out of fear and obligation, you are giving your power away. Every time you walk into the room and see it, your energy levels drop.

And don't think "out of sight, out of mind" will work. You can't keep something in the cabinet and just bring it out when Aunt Jane is due to visit. Your subconscious mind still knows it's on the premises. If you have enough of these unwanted gifts around you, your energy network looks like a sieve, with vitality running out all over the place.

Remember, it's the thought that counts. You can appreciate being given a gift without necessarily having to keep it. Try adopting a whole new philosophy: when you give something to someone, give it with love and let it go. Allow the recipient complete freedom to do whatever they want with it. If the most useful thing they can do is put it straight in the trash or give it to someone else, fine (you wouldn't want them to clutter up their space with unwanted gifts, would you?). Give others this freedom and you will begin to experience more freedom in your own life, too.

THINGS YOU DON'T LIKE

These are things you bought yourself, but have never really liked since the day you got them. Usually you are keeping them until you have the time or money to buy something better.

I'll give you an example. I've never liked ironing very much. I had a perfectly good, average kind of iron but I was never inspired to use it. I went to great lengths to make sure I hardly ever wore anything that needed ironing. Then one day, while staying at a friend's house, I discovered what I can only describe as "the empress of irons." True, it cost twice as much as the run-of-the-mill item I had at home, but what a joy to use. It took ironing to a whole new level I never knew existed. When I got home I went straight out and bought one, then spent a whole afternoon contentedly ironing my way through all my clothes. For the first time in my life I experienced this activity as a pleasure.

Don't put up with giving yourself second best. When you nourish yourself by giving yourself the best you can, that signal goes out and will attract the best in other areas of your life, too. If you are struggling financially and just "getting by" with most of the things you own, love them, be grateful for what you have, and intend to soon create the resources to replace them with things that inspire you more. Most people are surprised how quickly this becomes possible once they set their intention to do it.

THINGS THAT NEED FIXING

Things that need fixing are an energy drain. This is because everything you own comes under the mantle of your care and protection. You may conveniently put off doing anything about it, but your subconscious mind keeps track of these things, and every time you see the object or one that reminds you of it, your energy drops.

Suppose you have a chair with a wobbly leg. You have long since tuned out consciously seeing it when you walk into the room, but your eyes do still see it, your subconscious mind does still register it, and your body never fails to react energetically. When you promise yourself you will repair something and then don't, you lose even more energy and vitality from your body.

One woman I know lives in a big house where just about everything in it needs fixing in some way. She does admittedly live on a low income and has a child to support, but she is a resourceful, capable woman who could fix things if she wanted to. The lack of care and respect that she has for her home reflects the lack of care and respect she has for herself. When you care for your home by looking after it, you are loving and respecting yourself.

Think of repairing and improving things in your home as an investment in yourself. And if there is something you can't be bothered to fix, then find it a new home with someone who would like it and is willing to repair it, or get rid of it in some other way.

DUPLICATE CLUTTER

I once did a consultation for a clutterholic spinster whose even-more-clutterholic parents had died and left her everything they had in their home. So she had two sets of kitchen equipment, two sets of bathroom equipment, two sets of living room furniture—two of everything, all crammed into her house. In fact, she had three of four of some things. And there just wasn't room. However, she couldn't bring herself to throw anything away because most of the items still had years of use in them. Her home became so energetically clogged that it was literally difficult to breathe in there, and her whole life ground to a standstill while she continued the arduous task of sorting through all the crates of inherited household items and personal belongings.

Check through your belongings and count how many of each

type of thing you own. If you have lots of space, it's fine to keep some extras, but if not, it's time to do some thinning out.

INHERITED CLUTTER

Many people feel obliged to keep items out of respect to the memory of someone who has passed on. But the thing to remember is that whoever gave it to you is now in Spirit, where there is no attachment to the material world. The person will totally understand your need to let it go if it's holding you back. Give yourself permission to do so if you want to. If you don't love it or it isn't useful, let someone else inherit it from you right now.

One reader wrote to me to say:

> "Your book has made such a difference in our lives! Thank you! We bought copies for all of our family members and just this morning I got a call from my mother saying how much she appreciated it. She now feels ready to move on after her husband's death."

Then there is the other side of the coin. If you don't clear your clutter before you die, what burden will you be leaving your family and friends when you go? Unless, of course, you are thinking of leaving the type of inheritance described in the next letter . . .

> "After having read your book I decided to clear out my grandmother's house I was now living in. Trust me when I say that the family didn't like my clearing and getting rid of all of their 'mommy's stuff.' As I was going through

old trunks, I found over $5,000 wrapped up in an old handkerchief. This got the family's interest and they all descended. We cleared out everything and found nearly $8,000 in total that was hidden over the years."

For a deeper understanding of what happens after death, read *Death, the Great Journey* by Samuel Sagan, which is produced in the form of a Knowledge Track and can be ordered at the clairvision.org website (it comes in audiobook format, with an accompanying PDF that can be printed out, if preferred). I rate this as the most important book I've read this lifetime, and I highly recommend you get a copy. It's totally inspiring, and will give you a profoundly insightful perspective, not just on death, but also on life. You will certainly reconsider any attachment you have to clutter after reading it!

BOXES

I'll never forget the surprised look on the face of a furniture removal man as he bent to lift one of my large boxes that he expected to be as heavy as all the other ones he had been lifting all morning—and toppled over on his back. That was in the days when I was still a secret collector of empty boxes!

Personally, I find boxes immensely satisfying and reassuring. Often I am more delighted by the box a present comes in than the present itself. But this can be a very space-consuming passion, and in terms of the feng shui bagua, it is not exactly energizing to have "empty box" energy concentrated in any part of the home. It brings a hollow feeling to whatever aspect of your life that part of the bagua represents. I now strictly limit the number of empty boxes I have and make sure that most of them are put to good use rather than idling empty about the place.

When you purchase new equipment, keep the box it came in for the duration of the initial warranty period and then get rid of it. Don't keep the box forever "just in case" you move and need the box to pack it in. It is perfectly easy to pack equipment in standard moving boxes when the time comes.

Another useful tip if you do have to keep boxes for any reason is to open them out and store them flat. They take up far less space this way and don't have that "empty" energy anymore.

MYSTERY ITEMS

Everyone has a few of these, especially in the junk drawer. They include unidentifiable spare parts you have kept for years, wall-mounting brackets for pieces of equipment you will never mount or no longer own, strange widgets and rubber thingamajigs that fell off something but you don't know what, and the list goes on. All prime candidates for clutter clearing.

13

The Big Stuff

While you are clutter clearing, don't forget the BIG stuff. That horrible old piece of furniture you have always hated, the grand piano clogging the living room, the rolled-up rug you never use, the car rusting in your backyard, the ragged ten-year-old Swiss cheese plant gathering dust in the corner.

Some of these things are so big and moving them such a challenge that you learn the art of seeing through them as if they no longer exist. You may be able to do this indefinitely but like it or not, the bigger they are, the more they clog your energy flow and the more important it is to get them off the premises. This is especially true if their symbolism is actively impeding your progress in life. A rusting car in the Prosperity area of your garden is sure to affect your finances; a battered-looking plant in your Career area will make you feel tired and lethargic about your work or your life; useless furniture in any area of your bagua will create obstacles in that area of your life; and so on.

Maybe it's not that you have accumulated oversize junk so much as that your home is simply too small to accommodate it. This often happens if you move from a large home to a smaller one and try to bring all your furniture with you. Or maybe you have accepted gifts of furniture or collected things for when you move to a bigger place. In these cases you need to make a realistic assessment and a practical trim-down. When your home is so full of stuff that there is virtually no room for people, you will feel stifled in your choices. Clearing some space will allow new opportunities to blossom.

Search the Internet and you'll probably find someone who'll be delighted to come and take away your outsize junk, and possibly even pay you for the privilege. Or join the Freecycle Network at www.freecycle.org, the largest recycling and reuse website in the world. It's a grassroots nonprofit organization that invites you to "give or receive what you have and don't need, or what you need and don't have." Its motto is "changing the world, one gift at a time"—big stuff, small stuff, any stuff. Freecycle has millions of members in branches all over the world.

If the Internet doesn't help you shift all your oversize junk, you may have to pay someone to take it away, or get your friends and family to help you dismantle it and take it off for recycling or to your local dump. After it's gone, you'll be delighted at the difference and wonder how you ever lived with it for all those years!

14

Other People's Clutter

You can take a lot of liberties with your family, friends, and colleagues, but just lay a finger on their clutter and you will soon see some sparks fly!

One of the questions I am most frequently asked is what to do about other people's clutter—especially the clutter of people you live with.

CLUTTER ISSUES BETWEEN PARTNERS

Merely discussing your partner's clutter with them can quickly bring to the surface issues that have long been buried in a relationship. Nagging, arguing, threatening, and issuing ultimatums only makes clutterholics more entrenched, and NEVER, EVER, EVER clear their clutter for them unless they specifically ask you to do so. People have deep emotional attachments to their junk and can get very upset or even go berserk if it is tampered with.

Understand that you can never change anyone else. The only person you can ever change is yourself. In all the years I have been teaching this material, there are only two remedies I have consistently found to be effective in dealing with other people's clutter: education and leading by example.

Education

People really need to understand the downside of clutter if they are to have any incentive to do something about it. This is why they often reappear at one of my workshops several months later with a partner in tow, specifically for that person to hear what I have to say. Part of my reason for writing this book is to reach more of these partners and avoid the need to drag them along to hear me speak.

Leading by Example

I have heard from a significant number of people that as soon as they start clearing their own clutter, members of their family and close friends, without any prompting, suddenly take it into their heads to do the same. In many instances there isn't even any verbal communication between them. Somehow the message goes down the wire to the people they are on the closest frequency to, even if they live at a distance.

One memorable story was told to me by a woman who had read my book and enthusiastically began clutter clearing her home. The process took her the better part of two weeks. During that time her grandfather, whom she hadn't been in contact with for a while and who lived over two hundred miles away, stunned his entire family by unexpectedly clearing out forty years of junk from his garden shed.

Another woman took a weekend workshop with me in London. While she was there getting this information about clearing clutter, her husband spontaneously decided to have a huge clear-out and spent the whole day carting six carloads of clutter to the dump!

This has actually become a common occurrence at my "Clear Your Clutter" workshops—there are always some participants who report that, while they were sitting in class, someone at home or someone they know very well suddenly got inspired to clear some clutter.

A woman I trained as a space clearing practitioner once gave me a wonderful insight into clutter issues between partners. She naturally lived a very tidy and clutter-free life, and her husband's ever-messy desk really started to bug her. She knew that because the desk was in her life it must somehow be reflecting a part of herself, but try as she might, she couldn't figure out how that could be. Then one day she suddenly got it. She realized that although her husband was messy on the outside, he was very ordered and organized on the inside; she, on the other hand, was ordered on the outside but not as organized on the inside. And then what happened? Soon after she had this realization, her husband spontaneously decided it was time to tidy up his desk and keep it that way!

CHILDREN'S CLUTTER

Where does it all come from? Children's clutter seems to breed and take over space at an alarming rate if it is not checked and controlled.

One of the most important things to instill in a child is confidence. When children feel loved, secure, and happy, they don't have such a reliance on "things." Empower them by instilling clutter-consciousness at an early age so they don't become the clutterholics of the future.

Start by teaching your children to pick up after themselves. When they get a new toy, decide together where its storage place will be so they know exactly where to put it away when they're done playing.

Periodically get them to make decisions about toys they have outgrown—which to keep and which to give away. Let them make the final decision, though. Something that may look to you as if it's died and gone to heaven may still have huge importance and years of usefulness for your child.

Childhood hoarding can stem from a number of factors. If your offspring seem untamable, realize that all children act out the subconscious minds of their parents, so if you find yourself repeatedly nagging them, you will get better results if you work on your own clutter issues first. In other cases, hoarding is a coping mechanism for some kind of trauma a child has experienced, and a cry for help that needs to be heard.

Here's an inspiring letter I published in the Readers' Letters section at spaceclearing.com from someone who describes herself as a clutter-hoarding pack-rat princess:

> "I'm nine years old and I used to be a total pack rat! I used to fit in three-fourths of the clutter-hogging reasons—the 'just in case' items, identity, territorialism and 'scrooge-ness.' I used to keep every letter, receipt, movie stub and clothes that didn't fit me. I was mad when my old clothes got passed down and sad when I threw stuff away. I'd just like to thank you for writing your book so that I and many others could be free!"

TEENAGERS AND CLUTTER

With all that hormonal stuff rocketing around in their bodies, it's understandable that keeping their rooms tidy or clutter-free isn't exactly high on the list of adolescent priorities. Unless they got in the habit of living clutter-free when they were younger, they probably feel they have quite enough to cope with, thank you very much. Teenage clutter and chaos is usually their inner turmoil showing up on the outside.

I once appeared on a phone-in for a music show on MTV, answering questions from young people about how to use feng shui in their lives. The three main topics they wanted help with turned out to be passing exams, making friends, and getting their parents off their case. Most teenagers feel the need for emotional and physical privacy to a greater or lesser degree, and parents need to respect this, just as teenagers also need to respect their parents' space. However, it is reasonable to ask teenagers to agree at least to confine their clutter and chaos to specific rooms and then straighten them up regularly.

CLUTTER BELONGING TO FRIENDS, NEIGHBORS, AND RELATIVES

Sometimes people don't have much clutter of their own but they agree to keep things for other people. "Please look after this ugly sofa for me while I visit New Zealand." Two years later you are still waiting for your friend to come back and the sofa has started to grow roots!

Think carefully before you agree to clutter your own space with someone else's stuff, and if you do decide to do it, at least set a time limit: "Okay, I'll look after your ugly sofa, but if you're not back for it within X months, it's firewood/will be used to stuff a thousand cushions for charity/or whatever." Make a clear agreement about what will happen to the sofa and when, and that way your friendship won't deteriorate if things don't go according to plan.

An Australian friend once told me how she stored her belongings for years while living abroad, paid $700 to move them during that time, and eventually made $60 from selling the whole lot. Realizing that most of the things people ask you to look after aren't worth the boxes they're stored in makes it a whole lot easier to feel okay about turning down their pleas for dumping space.

15

Clutter and Feng Shui Symbology

One of the greatest incentives for getting rid of clutter is understanding that keeping the stuff is doing you no good at all.

There are two ways that the symbology of the things in your home can affect you. The first stems from negative associations you have with something, and the second has to do with the frequency emitted by the object itself.

NEGATIVE ASSOCIATIONS

Personal Associations

If you have things in your home that have unfortunate personal associations, it doesn't matter if they still have years of serviceable life in them—they are cluttering your space and also your psyche.

Many years ago, I had a boyfriend who would kick things when he got moody, and one day my portable sound system got the boot. The relationship didn't last long, but I kept the sound system. Every time I used it, I saw the damaged bit on top and remembered the incident that had caused it, but I kept it because it was still perfectly good otherwise. This went on for about a year until one day I looked at it, remembered the incident, and decided I didn't want to be reminded of it ever again. I realized that it had become symbolically associated in my mind with being disappointed by men.

I went straight out, bought a new sound system, and gave the old one to a girlfriend who needed one. She was very happy. She had no idea why there was a bit of plastic missing off the top and didn't care because a slightly imperfect-looking sound system was a whole lot better than no sound system at all. For me, however, the negative association I had with it caused my energy to sink every time I saw it, and it felt wonderful to be rid of it. I started attracting a much better quality of men into my life, too!

Outdated Associations

Sometimes personal associations are not negative, just outdated. For example, when I am called in to do a consultation for someone who wants to create a new relationship, I go around the home and often discover many things that belonged to, were gifts from, or still remind the person of a previous partner they haven't quite let go of. Whether they are conscious of the association or not, their energy is constantly being tugged back to the past, and it makes it very difficult to create anything new.

If, say, 50 percent of your furniture and belongings are associated with a time in your life you want to move on from, then 50 percent of your energy is tied to the past rather than available in the present. Try as you might, progress will be slow. Similarly, if your home is full of furniture, ornaments, or other items that constantly remind you of relatives or friends you've had difficult or uneasy relationships with, these associations will have an equally draining effect on you.

This also explains why you owe it to yourself to start any important new relationship in a place where neither of you has lived before. The odds are stacked against you if either of you has old associations with your home.

A deep and thorough space clearing ceremony will remove the old imprints but can do nothing about the mental and emotional associations that are triggered when you see familiar objects. One way to deal with this is to spend the time and energy forging new, stronger, happier, and more positive connections until you reach the point where you completely overwrite and unplug from the old associations. One woman I know painted all the Victorian furniture she had inherited from her grandmother bright blue and yellow to blend in with the rest of her decor, and that did the trick. As she painted, she actively infused the furniture with all the love and joy she could muster, and from that point on whenever she looked at it, that was the strongest association for her.

The other way to get rid of old associations is to dump the lot and start again, and twice in my life I have done this. Both times it was an incredibly scary yet wonderfully refreshing, regenerative experience, a real turning point. The circumstances called for it, but most people don't need to be so radical. Just gradually aim to replace the items you have the most unproductive associations with as you are able.

Frequencies

I've long had the ability to stand in front of a picture and feel its effect. Some time ago, I came across a book called *Life Energy and the Emotions* by John Diamond, in which he explains what is happening. For example, he shows a photograph of Winston Churchill with a particular expression on his face; the caption says, "Most people will test weak for the liver meridian when looking at this photo." Another photograph is captioned, "Most people will test weak for the heart meridian when looking at this photo," and so on, through all the meridians. He has worked out the negative and positive emotional states associated with each of the energy channels in our bodies.

Chinese medicine teaches us that we have twelve main pairs of meridians through which energy moves around our bodies, and acupuncture is based on harmonizing and rebalancing the flow of energy in these meridians to revitalize the relevant organs they are connected to. John Diamond's research concludes that the function of these energy channels, and thus our general state of health, is very much influenced by positive and negative emotional states. For instance, he says that the liver is weakened if you feel unhappy and strengthened when you switch to feeling cheerful; the heart meridian is weakened by anger and strengthened by love and forgiveness; the spleen is weakened by anxiety about the future and strengthened by an attitude of faith in the future. It's a fascinating study and the book is well worth a read.

What really grabbed me about it, though, was its application to feng shui. I've been on many a consultation where I have found, in a prominent position in someone's home, a picture, photograph, painting, poster, statue, or other object that is emitting a frequency totally counterproductive to everything the client has told me they want. One woman had a huge, mournful portrait of herself, painted in dark, somber colors, positioned in the most dominant place in her living room, next to the doorway that led to the kitchen. She must have seen that portrait a hundred times a day, and I knew immediately from the way it affected my body that she must be depressed. It had cost her so much money she was loathe to get rid of it, so I persuaded her to at least take it down for a month or so and see how that felt. She was astonished at how much better she felt without it and never hung it up again.

The photo of myself on the back cover of this book will raise your energy when you look at it. It was specifically created with this in mind, and the feedback I have had from people of many different cultural and social backgrounds confirms this. They all say to me, "I just looked at your photograph and knew I wanted to know more about what you do." This type of feng shui symbology is universal in its application.

Arranging Your Home for Symbolic Effect

Go around your home, look at all your belongings, and ask yourself, "What is this saying symbolically? How is it affecting me energetically? Is it creating the effect I want, or could I do better?"

Begin by culling things that pull your energy down, such as a predominance of downward-hanging things (plants, decorative items, and so on). This is particularly important if you have low-ceilinged rooms, where your energy is squashed before you even begin.

Next, start counting. Do you have things arranged singly, in pairs, or in groups? If all your ornaments are solitary, life will tend to dish up solitary experiences. If you'd rather be partnered, tweak the energy of your home by arranging things in pairs. Happily married people naturally buy two of everything because it feels right (ask some and see!). If you are single, it may at first feel strange to do this because you have been used to being solitary. You will need to keep doing it until it feels like second nature, which will create the shift in your own personal energy that you are looking for.

Then look at the symbology of your home in the context of the feng shui bagua. Check that each area of your home, and each area of each room of your home, has appropriate symbology that supports you in what you want to do in your life.

I remember one client who told me she was always arguing with her employer, and there in the Career area of her home was a huge oil painting of a battle scene. Another client, an illusionist, was very successful but had difficulty actually getting paid for the shows he performed. It turned out he kept all his trick mirrors and trick money in the Prosperity area of his house.

Start to look at everything in your home and ask yourself, "What does this symbolize to me and how does it make me feel?" Then move on to the detailed explanation of how to clear clutter in the next part of this book, which will help you sort through your belongings much more easily.

Part

3

CLEARING
CLUTTER

16

How to Clear Your Clutter

Here are three tried-and-true ways to deal with your clutter:

1. The Let-Nature-Take-Its-Course Method (also known as the Abdicating-Decision-Making Technique). Put clutter in a place where it will disintegrate to such a point that you no longer want to keep it. One man I met, who was on an extended vacation far from home, confided, "I cleared out a lot of clutter and put the rest in an outdoor shed. I am hoping that by the time I get back it will be so mildewed I will have to chuck it out."

2. The Wait-Until-You-Die-and-Let-Your-Relatives-Sort-It-Out Method. This has been a great favorite throughout the centuries. You can even draw up a will telling people exactly what to do with it all!

3. Take Responsibility for the Stuff and Clear It Yourself. This approach is far more empowering, has much better karma, and allows you to get on with your life immediately instead of waiting for you or your clutter to expire. It is the method I recommend.

GETTING STARTED

Without a doubt, people find that the hardest part is overcoming their inertia enough to get started. Once they have begun, the process itself releases more energy to continue. All the stagnant energy that is locked up in the clutter becomes available for you to use in more positive ways. And the more you clear clutter, the easier it becomes, because you know how good it feels after you have done it and you know the positive benefits that follow.

My general rule of thumb is that if I were moving tomorrow and would have more than one or two trash bags of stuff to throw away, I've got some sorting to do right now. I live like this because my life works so much better. It is not a discipline I have to practice—it just makes so much sense to me that I wouldn't want to live any other way. And it isn't something I am fanatical about—I just put a bit of time into sorting things on a regular basis so that everything stays manageable.

So here are some pointers to get you started on your Great Clutter Clear-Out . . .

Handling Your Thoughts and Emotions

In this book I'm not telling you that you "should" do this or "should" do that. My intention is to explain how keeping clutter can affect you so that you can make your own informed choices.

"Should" is one of the most disempowering words there is. When you use it, you feel guilty and obligated. My advice is to dump the word from your vocabulary forever. Use "could," not "should," from here on in.

Feel the difference: "I should start clearing my clutter today" or "I could start clearing my clutter today." "Could" empowers you, gives you choice, and later allows you to take the credit for a job well done. "Should" depresses you, makes you feel at fault, and brings you little joy on completion of the task.

I suggest you also dump "can't" and substitute "won't." Then you'll really make some progress. Again, feel the difference: "I can't decide whether to keep this or let it go" or "I won't decide whether to keep this or let it go." In the "can't" example, you are helpless and hopeless. In the "won't" example, you are expressing your decision as a being of free choice, and if you then ask yourself why you won't let it go, you will discover it comes down to some subconscious block you never realized you had: "I won't decide whether to keep this or let it go because it brings up all the feelings to do with my mother/father/spouse . . ." and so on. Well, you still have work to do, but at least you're being honest now.

The Best Time to Clear Clutter

Any time is a good time. Since most clutter clearing is done indoors, you can do it day or night, any time of year, come rain or come shine. However, if you happen to be reading this book in the spring, this timing will get you off to a good start. There is a natural instinct to have a good cleanup at this time of year, when there is new growth and emergence in nature. If you live in a part of the world where there are only two seasons (wet and dry) rather than four, you will find it easier to have a clear-out at the beginning of either period.

Another good time is just after you get back from a vacation. You have a different perspective at these times and it makes it easier to make decisions about what you realistically need to keep. The same is true when you move, recover from an illness, start a new job, begin a new relationship, or make some other major change. But don't make waiting for one of these things to happen an excuse for not beginning. I repeat, any time is a good time!

I generally recommend at least one major clutter clearing every year, and if you really want your life to work well, then it needs to be under constant review. Clear the bulk of your clutter first and then keep it manageable thereafter.

Doing It Fast or Slow

People have different amounts and types of clutter, not to mention different levels of willingness to let it go. I find that they approach clutter clearing in one of two ways: one type of person will read this book, cancel all appointments, and ninja through their home like a white tornado, decluttering with glee; the other type will do it in stages.

If you need more time, just accept that you do. It may be that you are too busy, too stressed, or just too overwhelmed by the sheer amount of your clutter. Progress at your own speed, whatever that may be, and do a bit at a time as you feel able. However, bear in mind the following:

If you are busy—remember, you *do* somehow find the time to acquire the clutter so you *can* make time to get rid of it!

If you are stressed—know that clutter clearing is one of the best therapies there is for worry, stress, and anxiety.

If you feel overwhelmed—you won't be if you follow these easy steps, which have already helped millions of people lighten their load, including many who are far more entrenched clutterholics than you (you wouldn't have made it this far in the book if you were that bad a case).

Make a List

First, take a tour of your home with notepad and pen in hand, noting down the clutter zones in each room. If you are not at home (or are lazy!), just close your eyes and imagine yourself walking from room to room. Most people find they know exactly where their clutter is.

Then take another piece of paper and rewrite the list, beginning with smaller clutter zones at the top and working your way down to monster mounds.

Examples of small zones are behind doors, individual drawers, the bathroom cabinet, small chests, briefcases, toolboxes, etc.

Middle-size zones are clothes closets, kitchen cabinets, linen closets, desks, filing cabinets, and so on.

Large zones are junk rooms, basements, attics, garden sheds, garages, and any clutter-filled spaces that clearly will take longer to conquer.

Now put an asterisk beside the zones that irritate you the most. These are the ones to begin with, going from small to large. Get some small successes under your belt first and then you will be inspired and encouraged to tackle the bigger areas later. And when you feel how good it feels to tackle the clutter zones that really bug you, you'll be more motivated to wade into those bastions where you wish the clutter would just melt away of its own accord.

Motivate Yourself

Another strong motivator is to use the feng shui bagua (see chapter 8) to check which areas of your life you have been sabotaging by piling junk in that area of your home. Most people are amazed to discover how accurate this system is. Then give some thought to how you would like this aspect of your life to be in the future. Bearing this in mind really helps to get you started and keep at it until the job is done.

Space Clearing to Help Clutter Clearing

This book is intended to so motivate you to clear your clutter that it will be all you need. However, if you have a lot of stuff or don't feel quite motivated enough, doing a full space clearing ceremony will help you enormously to get started. It's ideal if you can clear the clutter first, but if you have serious amounts of work to do in this department, skip that part of the space-clearing preparations and do the rest of the ceremony to get the energy in the space moving.

Later, after you have cleared the clutter, you will be a different person, so you will need to do a second space clearing to refrequence your home to match the new you. But don't be put off by the thought of having to do the ceremony twice. As everyone with clutter knows, the difficulties it causes make everything in life harder to do, so it will come as no surprise that this includes space clearing. A space clearing ceremony is the fastest way I know to release the stagnant energy that accumulates around clutter, and when you discover how much this helps you clear out your junk, you won't mind doing the ceremony more than once.

For a detailed description of how to do space clearing, go to www.karenkingston.com to find my most recent book on this subject.

Final Preparations

By now you have an idea of how much clutter you intend to clear, so you must create some means of getting it off the premises. Unless you have already decided to order a Dumpster and go for it big-time, then simply have some cardboard boxes and/or trash bags at the ready. These will be your little army of helpers.

Suppose you decide to use boxes. The basic four you will need are:

- **A Trash box** for out-and-out junk, destined for the garbage truck.
- **A Recycling box** for paper, plastic, and other materials that can be recycled. Release them back into the world so that they can be made into something useful.
- **A Transit box** for things that are on their way to somewhere else in your home (to another room, or to a space that hasn't yet been created for them because you need to clear the clutter there first).
- **A To-Do box** for items that need your attention in some way. Don't interrupt the momentum of the clutter clearing process to stop and do whatever is required. Just put the items in your To-Do box and jot a note in your To-Do book about them. If a task is time sensitive, add a reminder on your calendar, too.

Depending on what types of clutter you have, you may also need some or all of the following boxes:

- **A Charity box** for things to be donated to charities, libraries, schools, hospitals, etc.
- **A Selling box** for things you can sell.
- **A Gift box** for things you have decided to give to friends or relatives.
- **A Returns box** for things that need to go back to the people they belong to.
- **A Repairs box** for items that need repairing, altering, renovating, etc. Only put in here things you are sure you want and need, and set yourself a time limit for getting them fixed.

And until you gain experience at this, you will probably also need:

- **A Dilemma box** for things you still can't decide whether to keep or let go (more about this later in this chapter).

CLEARING YOUR CLUTTER

Begin small. Choose just one very easy area to begin with. A drawer, shelf, or small cabinet is ideal. Give yourself the satisfaction of crossing it off your list when it's done.

Most people find they feel pretty good after clearing one area, so they decide to do another, and maybe another. Each small area you clear releases energy for you to do more. Take it at your own pace, doing as much as you feel inspired to do at any one time. This may take you a few hours, a few days, a few weeks, or a few months, depending on how much you have to clear and how gung-ho you are to tackle it. Remember—the speed at which the positive changes will appear in your life is relative to the gusto and decisiveness with which your clutter is cleared.

When you've completed some of the smaller areas, move to the middle-size ones and finally the largest ones, but still break each area down into bite-size manageable chunks. Divide cabinets into separate sections and rooms into separate areas. You can work through your entire home in this way and gain confidence as you go.

Do not make the mistake of dragging everything out of your cabinets, piling it in the center of the room, and trying to sort out the whole lot at one time. I've never heard anyone with more than a trivial amount of clutter say that this method worked for them.

On the other hand, if your situation is that everything is already in the center of the room when you start, then the first thing to do is make sure you have enough storage space to put it all away. Then divide the pile into smaller manageable chunks and get to work on them, one by one.

Sorting Through Your Stuff

As you sort through things, do not create a pile of objects with the intention of deciding later where they will go. Pick up each object in turn and make a decision about it then and there. Does it stay or does it go? If it goes, put it in the relevant box (Trash, Recycling, Charity, Selling, etc). If it stays, but needs attention, put it in the Repairs box. If it belongs elsewhere in your home, put it in the Transit box, which is a great invention because it prevents you from getting side-tracked if you wander off to other parts of your home while you work.

Toward the end of each clutter clearing session, take your Transit box on a walkabout and relocate its contents in or near the places you have decided each item will now live. If any of these places are already full because you haven't cleared them yet, the items will need to stay in the box for a while, which is not ideal but may be the best you can do.

Make this whole process fun for yourself. Decide now that everything that takes up space in your home has to have a valid purpose for being there. Ask yourself, "Does it pass the clutter test?"

The Clutter Test

Decide what to keep by asking yourself these three questions:

1. Does it lift my energy when I think about it or look at it?
2. Do I absolutely love it?
3. Is it genuinely useful?

If the answer is not a resounding yes to question 1 and an equally resounding yes to either question 2 or 3, then what is it doing in your life?

Does It Lift My Energy When I Think About It or Look at It?

Recognizing whether you feel energized or not is the most reliable part of the clutter test. Your mind can fool around with you and invent all kinds of excuses so that you get to hang on to stuff, but your body knows the truth and never lies. Trust the feeling in your body.

Do I Absolutely Love It?

If so, does it really inspire me, or is it just "nice"? Do I already have enough of this type of item for my needs? In spite of how much I love it, does it also have sad associations in my life?

Is It Genuinely Useful?

If so, when did I actually last use it? When, realistically, am I likely to use it again?

The Dilemma Box

While you're learning the knack of clutter clearing, you may need to use a Dilemma box. When you come across things that you know constitute clutter but you truly do not feel ready to part with them yet, put them in the Dilemma box and then stash the box in the deepest, darkest recess of a closet. Make a note on your calendar at a future time—say, in six months—to check on the box. Try to remember what is in it before you open it. The chances are you will have forgotten, in which case it rather proves the point that you don't really need any of those things. Your life has gone on perfectly well without them.

You could even get a friend to open the box for you (choose the kind of friend who doesn't have clutter and finds it hard to understand why anyone else would). Anything you can remember and still feel you have a genuine use for, you can keep; everything else, your friend takes away to dispose of however he or she wants, and you never see the items again. If this feels too extreme for you, then just open the box and seriously review the contents again, bearing in mind that you haven't needed any of them for the entire time they've been in storage.

One woman told me she was so worried she might regret getting rid of something that she bundled it up in three large trash bags and slept with them in her bedroom for three nights. She figured that if there were anything in there that she would miss, she would have been out of bed in the middle of the night, rummaging through the bags to retrieve it. But she slept peacefully every night, and on the fourth morning she happily dumped the lot in her garbage bins and didn't miss a thing.

Tidying

If your clutter is more of the messy variety than things that need sorting and tossing, here's a very good way to learn to tidy your home and keep it that way.

Start in one corner of the room. Pick up any object at random that needs to be put away. Let's say it's a shirt. Start talking to yourself out loud in a kind of rhythmic chant, describing what you are doing. "I'm picking up the shirt and I'm walking to the drawer. I'm opening the drawer and I'm putting it inside." Then get some more items from the same corner. "I'm picking up the newspaper and putting it in the bin. I'm picking up the book and I'm putting it on the shelf." And so on.

All your sentences need to have a similar rhythm and be in two parts: dee-da-dee-da-dee-da and dee-da-dee-da-dee-da. It is this rhythm that carries you along and makes the task enjoyable and fun. Kids love tidying this way. It also means that your mental dialogue is already full, so you don't get stuck in your usual indecisiveness or bogged down in details. You just get into the rhythm and go with it. You start in one corner and work your way across the room until it is clear. With a bit of practice you can even get the words to rhyme!

GETTING CLUTTER OFF THE PREMISES

Don't do all that work and not take the final step of getting the clutter off the premises. This is a crucial part of clutter clearing.

Throwing Things Away. Clutter that is no use to anyone in any shape or form is the easiest and quickest to dispose of. Hire a Dumpster to take it away, drive it to the dump yourself, or put it out for the local garbage service to collect. It feels very satisfying to get trash out of your home as soon as you can.

Recycling. The next easiest option is recycling, and in many parts of the world this is now just as simple (and a lot more environmentally responsible) as throwing stuff away. An amazing number of things can now be recycled. A quick Internet search on the word "recycle" and the name of the object you are ready to send off to a new incarnation will usually yield results.

Gifting. Gifts to friends, relatives, charity shops, institutions, and other deserving causes generally take longer to dispose of. You may have to wait until you see a particular friend or pass a certain charity shop, school, library, hospital, etc. Posting the item to a website such as www.freecycle.org can speed up the process. But if you choose the gifting option, set a date (say, the end of this month or next), and make a deal with yourself that you will send the item off for recycling or consign it to the garbage heap if you haven't given it to anyone by then. Don't misunderstand me. I am wholeheartedly in favor of giving ex-clutter to people who will use and appreciate it, but my experience is that most junk designated as gifts just sits in boxes or bags and never makes it out the door. Until you have become experienced at clutter clearing, it may not be wise to allow yourself the luxury of gifting. Just get rid of it as fast as possible in the most conscientious way you can.

Returning Things. This can also take a while. You have to contact the people the items belong to and request, plead, or insist that they take them out of your space. Set a reasonable deadline and let them know that if they haven't collected the stuff by then, you will dispose of it in any way you see fit. Alternatively, you can mail the items or deliver them yourself.

Selling Items. This can take even longer because now you have to find someone who will pay money for your junk. It's generally not a good bet for a first-time clutter clearer, unless you have a bulk purchaser or decide to have a yard sale (an excellent idea). If you have just a few items to dispose of, eBay or Craigslist can be a good solution.

Exchanging and Bartering. This is even more difficult because now you are looking for someone who wants what you have and has something you want. Set yourself a deadline and if you haven't found the exchange or barter you want to make by that date, sell the item, give it away, throw it away—do anything but keep it.

Repairing, Altering, and Renovating. These options can take the longest time of all and are by far the least likely to happen. The chances are very strong that the items will still be unrepaired, unaltered, and unrenovated this time next year or, in fact, this time next decade. Be particularly wary of keeping obscure items you have convinced yourself you will someday transform into something useful, and items you are keeping until you have something to go with them to make them useful.

CLEARING CLUTTER GETS EASIER THE MORE YOU DO IT

Like learning anything else in the world, clutter clearing is a skill that you can develop. Think of yourself as needing to build your clutter clearing "muscle." The more of it you do, the more proficient you become and the easier it gets, but when you first begin you can feel like a clutter clearing weakling.

After a few successes, when you experience what I call the E-factor of clutter clearing, it changes from being a chore to being a delight. "E" in this case stands for exhilaration—the joyful feeling of accomplishment you get when you finish a job.

One of my clients who had been a hoarder all his life became so enthusiastic about clutter clearing that he told me he would sometimes come home from work, say hello to his wife and children, and then go upstairs to his bedroom, open a drawer, select something such as a pair of old socks, and just for the sheer heck of it, throw them away! He'd discovered the E-factor.

Here's a personal example from my own life. I once set myself the goal of taking an early morning walk to a certain place, farther than I usually go. I got tired before I got there and nearly convinced myself to quit and go home. But instead I ignored the dialogue in my head and just kept walking until I reached my destination. A small goal, you may say, and seemingly unimportant, but the level of exhilaration in my body as I walked back was completely out of proportion to the achievement. I felt fantastic, and the feeling lasted throughout the day.

It's exactly the same with clutter clearing. You decide to clear a small drawer, and once you do it, the feeling of exhilaration that follows is almost heady. All kinds of energy blockages are released in your body, all the failures of previous attempts at clutter clearing are overwritten, and you feel unstoppable.

Actually, you can experience this any time you decide to do something and then do it. It's not limited to clutter clearing. The E-factor is one of the main things that inspires successful people to do more.

Treat Yourself

My whole intention in writing this book has been to make the benefits of clutter clearing so attractive that you will overcome the inertia of keeping your junk. Adopt the attitude that clearing out your clutter is a treat. Later, when you have experienced the benefits, you will want to treat yourself more often. As one woman said to me, "I never realized one could get just as much pleasure from getting rid of material possessions as from acquiring them in the first place!"

Remember, you don't need to aim for perfection. Just deal with the main items of clutter that are clogging up your space and then get on with your life.

It's Safe to Let Go

Affirm to yourself as you sort through your things, "It's safe to let go." Clearing clutter is about letting go and trusting the process of life to bring you what you need, when you need it. Anything you are keeping "just in case" you are keeping out of fear.

If you have a lot of clutter, you may need to go through it several times before you feel ready to let go of some things. In some cases, it may take a whole year or more before you finally admit to yourself that an object still hasn't come in handy.

SEVEN TOP CLUTTER CLEARING TIPS

Here are seven tried-and-true tips for effective clutter clearing.

1. Discover Your Most Effective Clutter Clearing Time of Day

Most people find they have a best time of day for clutter clearing. Some people prefer the morning. Others find it easier at night. Discover when you are at your most decisive and do your clearing then.

2. Schedule Clutter Clearing

Decide when you will begin and schedule it on your calendar, as you would any other activity. Make a date with yourself to do it, and show up. It can be a whole day, a half day, or a series of appointments of just an hour or half an hour, depending on how fast you want to progress.

3. Timebox Each Task

It's a well-known fact that all jobs expand to fill their allotted time limit, so if you tell yourself you will clear your stuff until it's done, don't be surprised if the process takes forever. Timebox each job. Break each task down into chunks, decide how long it will take you to complete each one, and then set your timer. Work against the clock to do each chunk within the timebox you have set yourself.

You can also use this technique to accomplish other types of tasks. For example, if you're doing a job at your computer, you might use one of the great timer software programs out there. Instead of a boring alarm sound when time's up, you can set the program to burst into life with any soundtrack you have on your computer. I revised and updated most of this book in sixty-minute timeboxes using this technique.

If you're the kind of person who procrastinates because you love the adrenaline rush of getting something done just in time for a deadline, you'll adore timeboxing. You won't have to wait for a big deadline but can get your fix many times a day. However, I have to warn you that with practice, you'll be able to timebox yourself without a clock, and will routinely start completing jobs on time. So use this technique only if the rest of your life is interesting enough not to need adrenaline highs (your kidneys will thank you for this and serve you longer because of it).

4. Play Upbeat Music

Some people prefer to clutter clear in silence, but many find they are able to keep going two to three times longer if they have the right music playing. If this works for you, be sure to use external speakers (not headphones) and set the volume loud enough to make your body feel like dancing. For best results, set your player to automatic repeat so that it just keeps going. Avoid alternating fast and slow songs—the ballads will cause you to lose momentum. If you have a lot of clutter to clear, it would be a good investment of your time to make your own music compilation especially for this purpose. But don't let doing this be yet another delay to making a start!

5. Wear Something Red

Just as red dancing shoes make your feet feel like moving, so does wearing red clothes make you feel like taking action. If you don't have anything red, then wear colors from the warm end of the spectrum (orange, yellow, etc.) rather than cool colors like blue. Many people keep clutter as a way of comforting themselves. Warm colors are more emotionally comforting than cool ones, so if you wear colors from the warmer end of the spectrum while sorting through your stuff, you'll probably find it easier to let things go.

6. Don't Wear Black or Gray

Black attracts low-level vibrations and will quickly make you feel tired when clearing clutter. Gray is also not a good color to wear because it can cause you to be indecisive about what stays and what goes.

17

Time Clutter

Many people get very inspired to clear their clutter after reading this book, but then find they are just too busy to put what they learn into practice.

We live in a busy world, where there seems to be less and less time. As Benjamin Hoff put it so eloquently in *The Tao of Pooh,* "If time saving devices really saved time, there would be more time available to us than ever before in history. But, strangely enough, we seem to have less time than even a few years ago. It's really great fun to go somewhere where there are no time saving devices because, when you do, you find that you have lots of time. Elsewhere, you're too busy working to pay for machines to save you time so you don't have to work so hard."

Physicists are not even sure time exists. They say that the passing of time may only be the way we perceive it, and that time itself may be an illusion, a matter of perspective. But it certainly seems real enough to us, and learning to handle it effectively is an important part of the clutter clearing process.

PRIORITIZATION

The first and most important step in tackling time clutter is prioritization. You need to establish your main priorities and arrange your life around them, not the other way around. Most people schedule everything first and then try to fit their life into the gaps in between. That's a surefire recipe for getting to the end of your days and realizing that you never figured out the important stuff or made time for it.

Prioritization requires a level of serious introspection that people generally find quite challenging, but it's really not such a big deal. In my experience of working with people over many years, the list of priorities doesn't vary that much from person to person. It's a matter of discovering what is important for you, while bearing in mind that priorities change as you move through different stages of your life. Being clear about your priorities enables you to maintain an overview so that you don't get lost in day-to-day details.

Establishing Priorities

So if I were to ask you now, what are the five most important things in your life, without which nothing else works, what would you say?

Perhaps you would immediately reply that your health and fitness is the most important thing, because without this it's difficult to do anything at all. Certainly if you have ever suffered with a chronic illness, had some kind of health crisis, or seen someone close to you go through one, you are likely to be especially aware how important good health is.

Or maybe you would say you value relationships most highly—your family, your friends, or one primary relationship you cherish above all else.

Or career. For some people this is at the top of the list, and relationships, health, and all other aspects of life get put on the back burner.

If you're reading this book, it's likely you are in a phase of your life where creating a home or work environment that supports and nourishes you has a high priority.

Or maybe for you the most important thing is acquiring wealth, financial freedom, travel, adventure, studying, pursuing an activity that you love, or something I haven't listed here. The main thing is to find what holds fire for you, what ignites you, what you are passionate about. Your priorities will emerge from that.

Note that I've left happiness off of the list. This is because it means so many different things to different people, as can be seen in the responses of a psychological test group (Emmons and McCullough, 2003), who were asked what they considered to be the greatest blessing in their life. Their answers ranged from "a healthy body" to "my mom" to "Instant Messenger."

Perhaps all the priorities I've listed so far are luxuries for you in your present circumstances, where the most important thing for you each day is to find enough food to eat, clothes to keep warm, and a safe place to be. Until you have the basic necessities of life, all other factors generally take second place.

But then again, perhaps you would say that even these are not the most important things. Food, shelter, health, loved ones, money, and everything else can vanish, but through all adversity, a person's spiritual path remains. Maintaining your spiritual practice may therefore have the highest priority of all.

Prioritization as a Daily Practice

Prioritization brings about a major clarification and simplification of your life. This is beautifully illustrated by a story about Charles Schwab, president of the Bethlehem Steel Company in America in the 1930s. He once employed a time management consultant, Ivy Lee, to shadow him for two weeks and then advise him on how he could improve his business. The report, when it came, consisted of just three recommendations:

1. Make a list of "Things to Do" every day
2. Prioritize everything on that list
3. Tackle things in order of decreasing payoff

"Don't pay me now," said Ivy Lee, knowing that this succinct advice was a far cry from the usual hundred-page reports Schwab received. "Just put my advice into practice for a month and then pay me what it is worth to you." The story goes that one month later, Schwab sent Ivy Lee a check for $25,000—an incredible sum of money in those days. His company went on to become the largest independent steel producer in the world, and in later life he declared that this was the most valuable piece of business advice he had ever received.

Whether you are a million-dollar executive or a suburban housewife, this advice holds equally true. Try it for a month and see for yourself!

Is the Jar Full?

To help you discover your own priorities, here's one of my favorite anecdotes that is said to have come from a talk given by Vice Admiral H. Johnson, who was the director general of the Indian Coast Guard in the late 1980s. To vividly illustrate his talk, he brought with him a transparent glass jar and proceeded to fill it with small rocks.

Having done this, he asked his audience, "Is the jar full?"

"Yes, of course," they replied, since it was clear not another rock could fit in it.

He then took a handful of tiny pebbles and threw them into the jar, filling the gaps between the rocks. Again he asked, "Is the jar full?"

"Now it is," they agreed.

Then he produced a bag of sand and tipped it into the jar, filling all the spaces between the rocks and pebbles.

"Is the jar full now?"

Finally he agreed with the group that it was full, and he explained how the jar is a metaphor for life. If you fill it with sand first (small details), it leaves no room for the pebbles (bigger issues). And similarly, if you fill the jar with pebbles first, it leaves no room for the rocks (your most important priorities). Life works only if you establish your priorities first and fit everything else around them.

In case you're interested, he listed his own top priorities as health and integrity. And if you want to take the metaphor a stage further, you can pour a cup of liquid into the jar at the end, analogous to the general smog of everyday life that everything is soaked in.

Getting Down to It

So again, what are your priorities? Seriously, don't go past this page without thinking this through. Stop reading right now and list your own top priorities in order of importance:

1.

2.

3.

4.

5.

In future editions of this book, I'd like to fix it so that the rest of the text vanishes until you've completed this exercise, but that technology doesn't yet exist. For now I'll just have to appeal to your greater wisdom to do it before reading on. If you've just read this paragraph without making your list, go back and do it!

Choices

Knowing your priorities is the only way to find your way out of time clutter. Otherwise, how will you ever decide what to say yes to and what to say no to? Life is a never-ending stream of choices to be made, and clear priorities will allow you to navigate through them rather than aimlessly drift or have things just happen to you.

Most people are so busy they couldn't cram another thing into their day if they wanted to. So forget about time management. That went out the day the electronic age was born. You are never going to have enough time to do all the things you need or want to do. Your only hope is to learn how to be selective, which quite simply means prioritizing from the top down, and learning to say no to low-value uses of your time.

Figure out the things you really enjoy doing and schedule them on your calendar before anything else. Don't allow your mental taskmaster to dominate your life. These pleasures are what your Spirit thrives on and if you just work, work, work without ever having time for yourself, or spend all your time looking after other people with no time to nourish yourself, pretty soon your enthusiasm for life starts to wither and die. The first signs of this are general fatigue and diminishing health. In planning your year, month, week, or day, schedule the activities that are important to you as a first priority and then fit everything else around them.

This is also very much in keeping with the Pareto principle I mentioned in chapter 9 (you get 80 percent of your results from 20 percent of what you do). The delicious implication of this is that you don't have to do four-fifths of all the things you think you have to do.

Prioritizing from the Top Down

At this point I want to introduce to you a concept that I teach to all the space clearing and clutter clearing practitioners I train. It's called Top Down, Zero Procrastination or TDZP for short, and sounds best pronounced as letters: "tee dee zee pee."

The TD (Top Down) part is what I've been talking about so far. Living life from this perspective gives you an overview. You position your consciousness so that you are always looking for how to invest your time in the wisest way and with the highest integrity. You see the bigger picture viewed from the top down rather than a narrow, blinkered view from the bottom up. Without this Top Down approach you will tend to choose the path of fastest, easiest gratification rather than the path that facilitates your highest priorities.

ZP (Zero Procrastination) refers to the immediate confirming action you take to ensure your life priorities are actualized, and are not just wishful dreams. ZP needs to become a way of life. Any time you catch yourself procrastinating, you need to shift to a Top Down standpoint and motivate yourself to action.

PROCRASTINATION

Do successful people procrastinate? Of course not! Successful people do what needs to be done, when it needs to be done, whether they like doing it or not.

Why Do People Procrastinate?

Many studies have been done on this topic over the years. One school of thought says that the main reason people procrastinate is that they fear failure so much, they don't even want to start. Other studies conclude that people put off doing things as an act of rebellion, because they feel the task is boring or unpleasant, or because there is no immediate reward from doing it. If you can identify which of these fits you most closely and watch out for it happening, your days of "blind" procrastination are nearing an end.

Then there are the people who are good at starting things but get easily distracted and put off finishing them. A hilarious version of getting distracted is "yak shaving," made famous by author and blogger Seth Godin. Yak shaving is defined as "any seemingly pointless activity which is actually necessary to solve a problem which solves a problem which, several levels of recursion later, solves the real problem you're working on." He gives an example of wanting to wax his car, but to do this he first has to buy a new hose, but to do this means he first needs to borrow his neighbor's E-Zpass to cross a toll bridge to get to Home Depot, but to do this he first needs to restuff the Moshi pillow his son borrowed from the neighbor. Hence ending up at the zoo shaving a yak!

Here's an example that nearly happened to me while writing this new chapter at my home in Bali:

> "I want to finish writing this chapter. To do this, I need to search the Internet for Seth's blog, *Don't Shave That Yak!,* so that I can quote his example."
>
> "Ah, but my broadband is not working today, so I'll need to use dial-up."
>
> "Hmmm ... the phone line is dead. The mice must have nibbled through the wires again."
>
> "Oh dear, the bamboo ladder I need to climb my garden wall to check the wires is broken."

And the next thing I know I've left my computer, loaded the broken bamboo ladder into my car, and spent the whole morning at the repair shop having it fixed.

Being wise to the perils of yak shaving, of course, I didn't do this. I used my neighbor's phone to call the broadband and phone companies to repair their services, sent my gardener to the repair shop with the ladder, skipped this paragraph until later, and continued writing.

How to Overcome Procrastination

My own observation of what lies at the root of procrastination is that it all comes down to will. Put simply, people of will get things done and people who lack will, don't.

And how do you build will? Well, that's one of those million-dollar questions, with no single or simple answer. Will has to be deliberately cultivated, a thousand times a day in every little way. Begin small and work your way up to great acts of will, which are sure to have a resounding effect in every aspect of your life. If this is your quest, an excellent starting point would be a wonderful little book entitled *Eat That Frog!* by Brian Tracy, subtitled *21 Great Ways to Stop Procrastinating and Get More Done in Less Time.*

Tracy explains, "It has been said for many years that if the first thing you do each morning is to eat a live frog, you can go through the day with the satisfaction of knowing that that is probably the worst thing that is going to happen to you all day long."

He adds, "It has also been said, 'If you have to eat two frogs, eat the ugliest one first' and 'If you have to eat a live frog, it doesn't pay to sit and look at it for very long.'" Of course, the book is not actually about eating frogs. They are just a metaphor for your most daunting tasks. But the vivid imagery that eating a live frog conjures up somehow works very well.

In my definition of clutter (see chapter 4), procrastination falls in the category of "anything unfinished," and like other forms of more tangible clutter, its effect on your energy is tiring. When you finally get moving and just do it, major reservoirs of energy are unlocked. You discover it actually takes more energy *not* to do something than to engage your will, roll up your sleeves, and get on with it.

Take correspondence, for example. Do you have letters or emails that you keep meaning to write but never get around to? Every time you think about the task and don't do it, your vitality levels drop. The longer you put it off, the more difficult it becomes to write the letter or send the email. If you just sit down and take the time to catch up on your mail, you will release huge amounts of energy for other purposes. It's the same with every procrastination you have in your life.

INTERRUPTIONS

Procrastination has been around a long time, but a new aspect of time clutter that we have to deal with in our modern, fast-paced world is the constant barrage of interruptions we're subjected to. Phone calls, text messages, emails, time pressures requiring multitasking, and the constant stream of interruptions from coworkers in most work environments means we are under constant stress to juggle all these things.

Studies led by Gloria Mark, professor of informatics at the University of California, Irvine, for example, have shown that IT workers are lucky to get three minutes of uninterrupted time to complete any task. She also found it takes an average of twenty-five minutes and two intervening tasks for employees to get back to what they were doing before being interrupted, and around 25 percent of tasks are not resumed at all the same day, if ever.

Interruptions cause a jarring in our energy that can be exhausting and debilitating. Some people cope better than others, but the continued assault on our senses to some degree affects our vitality, health, and well-being.

An experiment (Lefcourt, 1976) in which two groups of people were given complicated puzzles and a piece of proofreading to do while being subjected to an irritating noise sheds some light on why interruptions are such a problem. One group had a button that enabled them to turn off the noise; the other group did not. Not surprisingly, the group with control completed five times more puzzles and did a much better job of the proofreading than the group that had to put up with the noise. But very surprisingly, the group with the button never actually pushed it! As Howard Bloom commented in his book *The Lucifer Principle*, "It wasn't the noise or lack of it that affected their performance; it was the mere *idea* that if they'd wanted to, they could shut it off."

My husband, Richard, and I enjoy working together at home, usually on different projects. Realizing how irritating and nonproductive it is to be constantly interrupted by each other, we have developed a protocol that resolves this. Instead of asking questions or making comments whenever we want to, we first ask, "Can I interrupt?" It's remarkable what a difference this makes. By giving control to the person being interrupted, the whole jarring effect is radically lessened. We can say to each other, "yes," "not right now," or "wait a minute," and that's that. And if something is so critical that one of us has to interrupt urgently, we have found that a brief apology before doing so ("Sorry, but I need to know right now . . .") smoothes this over. Instead of feeling frazzled, we are able to take the interruptions in our stride. Studies conducted at the MIT Media Lab in Boston have found that polite interruptions by computers are similarly perceived as less intrusive.

Adapting this to a busy corporate work situation can be tricky, but certainly possible. Develop a system that lets colleagues know when you are working on something important and do not want to be interrupted (for example, close your office door, put a chair in the doorway, or put up a sign). Make it clear when you will be available, and do the same with emails and voice calls (use autoresponders and voicemail messages to inform people). Give an emergency access route when absolutely necessary and you'll find most people will adapt to your rules.

By planning your interruptions instead of having them constantly bombard you without any control, your productivity and job satisfaction will increase, and your immune system will not take such a pounding. In lab experiments, animals given control of their environment live longer, have higher antibody counts, and fewer ulcers. Your choice.

18

Staying Clutter-Free

One man sent an email to tell me, "I am busy clearing the clutter. Now I see more clutter than ever. I laugh at myself. I look in a drawer for something and see the mess. I stop and clean out the drawer. I feel better after each project is done."

Some weeks later he emailed me again: "I came in from a skiing trip last night and had four bags of stuff. Before I left this morning it all had to be put away because it was driving me nuts seeing the clutter."

This man has definitely integrated clutter clearing into his life. The knack to staying clutter-free is to change your daily habits.

A PLACE FOR EVERYTHING AND EVERYTHING IN ITS PLACE

I remember reading once about a very wealthy Arabian family who regularly traveled between four different cities in their country. The husband traveled to conduct his business, and his entire family accompanied him. Finding it very disorienting to be so much on the move, he used his wealth to build an identical mansion in each of the four locations, and had each home decorated and furnished exactly the same. Not only that, but when any member of the family went shopping for clothes, he or she purchased four of each item, one of which was sent to each of the different homes, to be hung in exactly the same place in each of the four identical closets. So no matter where they were, whenever anyone went to open their closet, it was the same.

As a frequent commuter between several destinations myself, I was fascinated by this description. An ordered home means an ordered mind. Whatever your personal situation, it is important to get organized so that the mundane level of your life works well and supports you.

GET ORGANIZED

One of the most amusing sights in the world is a myopic person hunting for lost glasses. After you have cleared your clutter from tabletops they will, of course, be much easier to spot, but make it really easy on yourself by allocating them a resting place all their own. Do the same with your keys, wallet, slippers, and any other items you find yourself continually searching for.

Here are some other organizing tips to simplify your life:

- Store similar things together.
- Keep things near where you are going to use them (for example, store your vases near where you arrange flowers).
- Put the things you use most often in places where they are easy to get.
- Make it easy for things to be put where they belong and then they won't get disorganized or cluttered.

- Label boxes so you know what is in them.
- Arrange your clothes according to color (they look much more appealing this way, too).

BUY A FILING CABINET AND USE IT

We live in the information age. Unless you have converted to an entirely electronic filing system, you need a place for keeping paper records, whether relating to home or business. The best way to deal with this is to purchase a filing cabinet. Some modern cabinets are very nice looking. You can store bits of paper that belong together in files and find them far more easily than if you keep them stacked in a pile. Create different categories and give them names that appeal to you. For example, would you rather file a document in your (yawn) Personal Savings Account folder, or would you rather file it in your (woo-hoo!) Go Anywhere Travel Fund?

If you find yourself with a piece of paper you need to keep and you can't figure out which file to put it in, don't just leave it in the unsorted pile—create a new category and a new file for it. Files that become suspiciously fat need to be either broken down into separate, smaller files or weeded of outdated documents. Files that stay persistently thin are either redundant or need integrating into larger ones. At least once a year, go through your filing cabinet and throw out anything that is no longer relevant.

STORING THINGS

The purpose of storage space is to hold things that are currently not in use. A good example is Christmas decorations, which are used only once a year. Winter clothes can be stored during summer months and vice versa. Then there are things such as camping equipment that are perhaps used only every other year. Just don't store too many things indefinitely without ever using them. That's when the energy starts to stagnate.

Some things you are obliged by law to keep for a certain amount of time, such as tax records and supporting documents. Find out the statutory requirement in your country. If it's, say, seven years, then file your papers in separate tax years so that as the new tax year dawns, you can easily locate your records from eight years ago and shred them. Most people find this tremendously satisfying.

STOPPING CLUTTER BEFORE IT STARTS

You can save yourself a lot of clutter clearing by adopting these new habits:

- ◆ Think twice before you buy. Decide before you purchase anything where you are going to keep it and what you are going to use it for. If your answers to either of these questions are vague, then you are about to purchase clutter. Desist from buying.
- ◆ Empty the wastebaskets in your home daily, either at the end of each day or first thing in the morning, whatever suits you best. Make sure you have one in each room that needs one so that when you want to throw something away you can, and they are big enough so they don't fill up so quickly you hesitate to put anything in them.
- ◆ Never put something somewhere "just for now." This means you are planning to go back to it again later and

put it in its proper place. Get into the habit of putting it in its place right away.

* If you know you are prone to accumulating clutter, make a new rule for yourself: When something new comes in, something old goes out. At least your clutter will be changing, even if it's not yet decreasing.

HIRE A PROFESSIONAL TO HELP YOU

I write my books to teach people how to help themselves, but maybe you have so much clutter that you really do need professional help to get you started and keep you going. In some countries (including the United States) you can hire people called professional organizers to help you tidy and organize your stuff.

The Level 1 clutter clearing practitioners I train are able to help you discover why you started accumulating clutter in the first place. Unless you understand this, you can tidy and organize things all you like, but the clutter will almost certainly build up again.

Level 2 clutter clearing practitioners are also space clearers. Through energy sensing with their hands, they are able to read the imprints that are embedded in your clutter and work with you at an even deeper level. They can also conduct a space clearing ceremony to clear the old imprints and the stagnant energy that has collected around the clutter. After that, it is so obvious what clutter needs clearing and so much easier to do it that it feels like the stuff could just walk out of the door by itself. They will teach you the skills and help you develop a plan to make sure it does.

You can find an International Directory of Practitioners who have trained with me at www.karenkingston.com.

19

Changing Standpoint

One of the greatest obstacles to clutter clearing is feeling too attached to items to let them go. But it's all a matter of standpoint, as this chapter will show.

WHY CHANGING STANDPOINT IS SO IMPORTANT

A journalist once interviewed me and we got talking about all the TV shows this book has spawned around the world. A typical format is to find someone with an incredibly cluttered home, drag all their possessions out onto their front lawn, and then film them going into emotional meltdown as all their stuff is carted away, never to be seen again.

What they don't show is what happens to these people after that. They don't show how traumatized most of them are by this, or how most of them start hoarding again to fill the emotional void left by the anguish of having all their stuff so quickly and radically stripped away.

I really don't believe this is the best way to help a hoarder, and when I published the first edition of this book in 1998, it was never my intention that this kind of televised spectacle would result.

The way to help people with clutter issues is to help them change their standpoint. They keep stuff because they believe they need it. Show them how to change their standpoint and their belief system about it can change, too.

A FRESH PERSPECTIVE

The things we keep around us reflect who we are.

One of the quickest ways to get a fresh perspective on your life is to take a good long look at everything in your home as if you didn't know the person who lives there. Better still, take photos of each room and look at the photos instead, which will give you more objectivity.

What would you conclude about the person who lives in this home? Is he or she the kind of person you want to know? The kind of person you want to be like?

It then becomes much more obvious what you want to keep and what needs to go.

LOOKING THROUGH NEW EYES

Start in any room and look at everything in it with new eyes. Which objects no longer fit with your life or with the direction you want it to take?

Perhaps you have some pieces of furniture you no longer use or like. Maybe you have some decorative objects that fit perfectly with your life when you first brought them home, but you've moved on, and they have not. What about your clothes? Weed out the ones you realize you no longer like or wear. Look at your bookshelves. Take out the books that are no longer interesting to you. Go through everything you own, discarding the items that no longer fit.

ARRIVING HOME AFTER A TRIP

It's even easier to get this fresh perspective in the first few days after you arrive home from a trip, especially if you've been away for at least a couple of weeks, and even more so if you've been abroad and spent time in a culture that is different from your own. You see your home in a fresh light. Things that have become clutter are so much more apparent than before, when you looked at them every day but didn't really "see" them.

It's a good idea to give yourself at least twenty-four hours at home after such a trip, rather than rushing back to work, or whatever your routine is, the next day. Give yourself the time to review your life and make the changes you want to make. This is when clutter clearing truly becomes a treat.

Arriving home from a trip is also a good time to sort through any photos you took while you were away. Look through them all, then keep the best and delete the rest right then and there before they even become clutter.

If you share your home with others who went away with you, they are likely to be able to see things more objectively, too, so invite them to be involved in the process. If they stayed at home while you went away, they may not see things the way you do, so in this case proceed gently, focusing on your own stuff and not even mentioning any of theirs. When you clear your own clutter simply because you want to, it has a delightful way of rubbing off on people close to you if you just get on with it and say nothing at all.

The important thing is to take the opportunity yourself before the fresh perspective of your trip wears off and you settle back into your old routines.

MOVING

Another good time to get a fresh perspective is when you move. Faced with the daunting task of packing everything to take it to a new location, it becomes easier to see what fits with your new life and what doesn't, what's worth taking with you and what isn't. You look at each item from a very different standpoint.

Some people, it's true, drag everything from one home to the next without sorting through or discarding anything. I remember one woman whose husband shipped all his clutter from the UK to their new home in Canada in a huge container, and there it sat in their garden, unpacked and unused for twenty years, until the time came to move back to the UK. When he announced he would be shipping the entire container back with them, she realized their relationship was over. From her standpoint, the twenty-year sojourn in Canada had more than proved the point that nothing in the container was of any use. From his standpoint, it was with him to stay, whatever the cost.

Even if you're not planning to move at the moment, you can make a tremendous shift in your relationship to your clutter by imagining that you are. Let go of everything you wouldn't consider worth paying a company to pack and transport for you.

IF YOUR HOME WERE ON FIRE

If your home were on fire and you had five minutes to rescue whatever you could, what would you take?

I sometimes pose this question toward the end of a clutter-clearing consultation after listening for hours to all the reasons why a client can't possibly get rid of this or that. They're so loaded with stuff they can hardly move in their home, but when asked what they'd rescue if the place were on fire, do you know what they say? Mostly that they'd save—*the cat*!

If they have a spouse or children, they sometimes (not always) say they'd save them first (maybe they figure humans can find their own way out of an inferno). Travel-oriented people often say they'd grab their passport. Some people have one or two prized possessions that immediately spring to mind. Other people want to rescue their photos. And after that, most really have to think about what else is worth saving. I call this the "moment of truth"—when they realize they don't really care that much about all their stuff after all. It all fades into insignificance. What's important is to get out of the fire alive.

People's relationship with their possessions really can be likened to a never-ending soap opera, with themselves as the star and all their stuff as the characters. When the scene changes from "normal" to "emergency," they suddenly see it all from a completely new standpoint, like awakening from sleep.

LETTING GO OF ATTACHMENT

A similar process happens as people approach death in old age. There is a gradual letting go of attachment to things as the realization dawns that you can't take any of it with you. Even the wealthiest, most powerful of people are subject to this. Death makes no exceptions.

Many people start to give away their things as the time of their death draws near. Some do this even if they have no way of consciously knowing it is imminent. Death creates an energetic opening that can clearly be felt, even if the person doesn't consciously understand it.

One of the most memorable examples of this was told to me by a friend some years ago. Her grandfather was attacked in his own home by a burglar and died as a result of his injuries, which saddened her greatly. But she drew great comfort from the fact that the previous week he had suddenly started giving all his most treasured possessions to his dearest friends and relatives. "It was as if he knew what was about to happen," she marveled.

Letting go of attachment to material things is a very important part of the death process. It's a time when we can see much more clearly that the world was here before we got here and will still be here after we leave. Material things have a degree of permanency. We are the transient ones. We're just passing through.

GET THE CLUTTER CLEARING KNACK

One of the main intentions of this book is to introduce you to a new standpoint about clutter. Before reading it you may have truly believed that all the things you were keeping were an asset in your life, but as you've turned these pages, you've learned about all the ways holding on to things can actually hold you back.

Having clutter tends to cause people to have small lives. There's no space for big ideas, inspired vision, or making a difference. They become stuck in their own world.

So what do you do if you've read everything in this book so far and still find it hard to let go of certain things? I'm a great believer in learning from others who've mastered a skill, so here's my best advice about this.

Find someone you like and admire who is not attached to their stuff. Talk to them. Find out how they think and feel about their possessions. Ask them to describe how they make their decisions about what they keep and what they let go of. Spend time with them as they go about their life.

See their viewpoint. Step into their mind-set. Adopt their strategies. Learn their knack.

Free yourself from the limitations of your own standpoint. You'll save yourself years of experimenting on your own.

20

Clutter Clearing Your Body

A natural progression of clearing clutter in your home is to clear the clutter inside the temple of your own physical body. People who collect clutter on the outside tend to collect it on the inside, too, but whereas clutter on the outside can hamper your progress in life, clutter on the inside can have more serious health-threatening or even life-threatening consequences.

The human body is a highly sophisticated processing machine. It takes stuff in, assimilates what it needs, and churns out the rest through five main eliminatory systems—the colon, kidneys, skin, lungs, and lymphatic system—and also several subsidiary systems such as the eyes, ears, navel, nails, hair, and in women, the vagina. All these channels are designed to efficiently remove the clutter of undesirable toxins from the body.

COLON CLEANSING

At the end of the "Clearing Clutter" chapter of my first book, I included a section entitled "Clear Out Your Colon." In just two concise paragraphs I outlined the principles of herbal colon cleansing and recommended a UK supplier of the herbal formulas I have used myself for many years with great results. I didn't contact the supplier to let him know I would be including his details and was amazed to hear a year later that he had been deluged with inquiries ever since from readers of my book. I am therefore including here a much longer and more complete section on this and related topics since there is obviously a lot more interest than I first thought.

Why You Need to Clear Your Colon

Most Western people don't even know that they need to clear their colon. They believe that the way they feel and the level of health they tolerate is the way things are, but in fact they no longer know what "normal" feels like. Years of eating unnaturally processed, cooked, frozen, canned, irradiated, and preserved food have contributed to this state. Undertakers report that corpses rarely need to be embalmed these days—we unwittingly eat so many preservatives that our bodies take much longer to decompose after death.

Curled up inside the human abdomen is about 22 feet of small intestine, leading to about 5 feet of large intestine, also known as the colon or bowel. So that you can visualize it, the large intestine is about 2.5 inches in diameter . . . or rather, it is supposed to be.

The first picture shows a healthy colon; the following pictures of unhealthy colons give examples of what can happen to people following a Western diet, which is well documented as being the unhealthiest in the world.

healthy colon

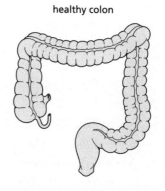

unhealthy colons

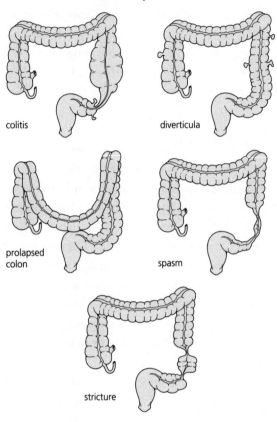

colitis

diverticula

prolapsed colon

spasm

stricture

It's likely that many of you reading this book have a colon that is distorted and coated in stagnant, impacted feces. Just about everyone who eats Western food does. Certainly if you have a thick waistline or bulging abdomen, this is very likely the case.

Mucoid plaque forms in the colon, partly as a residue of eating mucus-forming foods and partly because our bodies naturally secrete mucus in our intestines as a defense mechanism against toxins. The mucus can be cleared away by pancreatic juices, but mucus-forming food now forms such a huge percentage of the Western diet that the pancreas cannot cope. Layers of plaque build up throughout the length of the intestinal tract and then compact and harden.

With our modern-day child-rearing practices, this all begins when you are an infant. NASA research scientists have discovered traces of mother's milk in colons, indicating that many people carry impacted fecal matter in their colons all their lives.

A healthy colon contains residual friendly bacteria that weigh up to 5 pounds; encrusted colons have been found at autopsy to weigh 40 pounds or more. Sometimes there is so much putrid matter that parts of the colon expand from 2.5 inches in diameter to an obscene 10–20 inches in very obese people, leaving a channel of only about a pencil's width in the center through which excreted matter can pass. The colon becomes permanently toxic and all manner of health problems result as these poisons seep into your bloodstream and find their way to all parts of your body.

If you consume, or have ever consumed, meat, poultry, fish, dairy products, sugar, processed food of any kind, chocolate, caffeine, soft drinks, or alcohol, then you will certainly have mucoid plaque and will benefit from colon cleansing. Even vegans usually need to do it because of mucus buildup from soy and grain foodstuffs (soybeans are the most mucus-forming of all plants). All traditional cultures, whether meat-eating or vegetarian, have certain herbs they take from time to time to cleanse their intestinal tracts.

In the same way that each part of your home is connected to an aspect of your life, so each section of your colon is connected to a part of your body (see Dr. Richard Anderson's book, *Cleanse and Purify Thyself*). Hence many herbalists advocate colon cleansing as the cure for 90 percent of all diseases, and I certainly have found it to be enormously beneficial in terms of both preventative and curative healing. It works because not only do you clean up your internal sewer system, but in the process, all manner of emotional issues that may have been buried for years come to the surface and get released. It is in the emotional resolution that the real healing takes place.

Eating and Excreting

Eating and excreting is the most natural process in the world, yet most Western people are totally out of touch with their own bodies. In particular, they feel disgusted at the thought of their own excrement. I have noticed that Balinese babies get toilet trained much quicker than Western babies, and I think this is because they are not trussed up in diapers so they figure out what is going on much faster.

From all my research into this "not-to-be-discussed-in-polite-company" topic over the years, I have concluded that one of the dumbest things ever invented is the Western sit-down toilet. The squatting position adopted by the millions of people who live in the East opens the colon and makes it much easier to evacuate the bowel than sitting doubled up on a Western toilet. I think it is very likely this is a factor in why colon diseases are so common in the West and so rare in the East. (Note: A useful health tip if you use a Western toilet is to sit up straight and raise both arms high above your head—this opens up the intestinal tract in a similar way to squatting.)

Maybe this is all getting a bit much for you. I do appreciate how distasteful some people find these topics. However, I consider colon cleansing to be crucial to preventative medicine. If your colon is clear, your body thrives and your life works. If the colon is clogged, it will affect everything you do. If you need any more convincing, consider Dr. Richard Anderson's account of a very revealing experiment:

> Alexis Carrel of the Rockefeller Institute and two-time recipient of the Nobel Prize was able to keep chicken heart cells alive for 32 years by nutritious feedings and by washing away tissue excretions. The chicken heart cells grew and thrived as long as the evacuations were removed. Unsanitary conditions finally resulted in lower vitality, deterioration and death.

Constipation and Diarrhea

The general rule is, "new meal in, last one out," and researchers who have spent time in remote jungles around the world observing people who have an unstressed, natural way of life and healthy eating habits report that fifteen to thirty minutes is the usual time period between eating and excreting. So if you do not feel the urge to have a bowel movement within half an hour of finishing a meal, you are constipated. And long-term diarrhea is just as much of a problem because it means your colon is so laden with harmful bacteria (and probably parasites, too, which adore putrid, decaying matter) that it is constantly irritated.

The following symptoms also indicate colon problems: intestinal rumblings, stomach pains, smelly farts, feeling that even healthy food doesn't nourish you properly (poor nutrient absorption), bad breath, body odor, and smelly feet. You'll generally feel below par too.

If you are still in doubt, take the sunflower seed test. Put a handful of shelled sunflower seeds in your mouth, chew them as little as possible, and then swallow them. Now wait until they appear at the other end. If your intestinal transit time is about ten hours, this is good. If it's longer, you could use some colon cleansing to clear the encrustation. Some people find they have to wait three or four days before the seeds appear! One woman wrote to tell me how proud she and her husband were to notice the sunflower seeds emerging only twelve hours later . . . and then they noticed they appeared again and again over the next three days. So you need to keep watching.

The Ideal Poo

Now here is some information that is difficult to find in any book. Here's what an ideal bowel movement will be like after you have done thorough colon cleansing:

- Comes out easily and noiselessly within seconds
- Involves no straining
- Is light brown in color (unless you've eaten something like beets)
- Doesn't smell much
- Is soft and not compacted

This is why I say that reading material kept near the toilet is a sure sign of constipation—if you have time to read anything while you're in there, you're in bad shape!

The Benefits of a Clean Colon

So far I have outlined the dire consequences of a filthy colon; now here are some of the benefits of having a clean one. Most people find that after doing a colon cleansing once, they love the results so much that they make it an annual event. After this you can expect to:

- Feel and look healthier (better skin tone, fewer wrinkles, stronger nails, shinier hair, etc.)
- Feel more buoyant and energetic
- Have a stronger immunity to disease
- Derive more nourishment from your food and have less desire to eat junk food
- Experience more love, joy, and happiness in your life
- Be more flexible in your approach to life
- Be happy to let go of the old and welcome the new
- Enjoy more satisfying sex (because you do not have the internal pressure of an overburdened colon)

Louise Hay, in her book *Heal Your Body*, gives the metaphysical cause of bowel problems as "fear of letting go of the old and no longer needed," and recommends the affirmation, "I freely and easily release the old and joyously welcome the new." To reinforce this, when practical, start going to the toilet as soon as you feel the urge instead of waiting as long as possible, as so many people do. In this way you reeducate yourself to physically let go easily and quickly, rather than holding on to things until you are forced to act, and this filters through to mental, emotional, and all other aspects of your life.

Herbal Colon Cleansing

Herbal colon cleansing, done in conjunction with a regenerative nutrition program (there is no point in clearing junk out at one end while shoveling the same kind of stuff back in again at the other!) produces remarkable results. The program takes six to nine months, depending on how long you have been eating sugar, mucus-forming foods, or other junk food.

Never use laxatives. They irritate and weaken the bowel. Colonics are useful as an aid to cleansing the body during fasting but are no substitute for the deep cleansing and rebuilding properties of colon herbs.

It is always best to work with a qualified herbalist, and be sure to do so if you are pregnant, nursing, elderly, chronically ill, weak, or debilitated. The process invariably brings up emotional issues that you may need support with; you may also want reassurance when your body starts evacuating what looks like bits of old rubber tires. As one man told me, "It is horrifying to see what comes out but very satisfying to see it go."

Some excellent books I can recommend on this subject are *The Colon Health Handbook* by Robert Gray, *Dr. Jensen's Guide to Better Bowel Care* by Dr. Bernard Jensen, and *Sugar Blues* by William Dufty. You can find more information about these and other books in the bibliography. There is also a link on my website to a reputable supplier of Dr. Christopher's herbal formulas, which are the ones I have found to be the most effective.

Parasite Removal

There is a modern myth that worms and other parasites are found only in third-world countries. They also abound in the West, and colon cleansing is a vital part of clearing them from your body. If you read up on this topic, it may well be a revelation to you just how often parasites are implicated in poor health.

Fasting

After months of being "on the road" teaching workshops in the West, eating in restaurants, sleeping in hotels, and traveling on planes, it is pure bliss for me to get back home and have the time and space to do some honest-to-goodness juice fasting. Nothing revitalizes and energizes me more than fasting for a while on pure, organic, freshly juiced fruit or vegetables, and best of all, pure water.

Here's how it works. When you eat food, it takes a lot of energy for your body to digest it. When you fast on juices, all your internal organs get a vacation, so all that surplus energy is available for repair and revitalization. I believe the dumbest thing a person can do when they are seriously ill is to eat anything at all. Animals know this. They never eat when they are sick.

Except in medical emergencies, it is always best to do colon cleansing before juice fasting. Most of the unpleasant side effects people report from fasting are simply due to autointoxication from putrid matter caught in their own colon when it stops moving, and from impacted fecal matter that has been there for years. And for those of you who dread feeling hungry if you fast, here is a tried-and-true tip: for the first day or two, mix generous quantities of spirulina powder with your juice or take spirulina in tablet form (several dozen during the day). It is the most complete protein known, is excellent for toning the bowel, and you will hardly feel hungry at all if you take it. By the end of day two, most people find all hunger pangs have ceased.

The ultimate in fasting is the pure water fast. Again, except in medical emergencies, it is usually best to work up to this rather than taking just water from day one. Gradually dilute your juice more and more until you are drinking only pure water.

It is vital that you read widely on this subject before attempting a fast. You need to know how long to fast, what to fast on, and especially how to break a fast. Breaking one too quickly or with the wrong type of food can have serious, even fatal, consequences. However, done correctly, fasting is one of the most exhilarating experiences you can imagine. It is such a treat to give your internal organs a chance to rest and to experience what it is like not to stuff your emotions down with food all the time. You will discover new depths of passion and vitality in your life.

THE KIDNEYS

Our body weight is made up of approximately 70 percent water, and yet many people barely consume one or two glasses of pure water a day. All cells contain water—the blood is 90 percent water, and even our bones are 22 percent water. Its presence is fundamental to life and good health, to transport oxygen and other nutrients to cells and to take toxins away from cells.

So my message is: drink water. It is the best thing you can drink. Water cleanses and purifies, bringing you greater clarity in your life. Ideally, drink at least eight 8-ounce glasses of water a day. Freshly juiced fruit and vegetables are also good in addition to water. However, tea, coffee, sugared drinks, and alcohol put a tremendous strain on the body, especially the kidneys, liver, pancreas, and colon, and are to be avoided. They are largely composed of water but they also contain strong dehydrating agents.

You will know if you are drinking enough water by the very simple God-given mechanism called thirst. Do not ignore it. By the time you feel thirsty, your cells are already dehydrated. You can also check the color of your urine. Dark yellow urine means you are giving your kidneys a hard time. Very pale yellow or almost colorless urine means you are well hydrated.

There is also an art to when to drink fluids. It is best to drink about half an hour before you eat and then wait for one and a half to two hours after eating before you drink again. Otherwise you dilute the digestive juices in your stomach, which causes internal havoc (the food spoils and ferments, producing acidosis, which affects all body functions). When you chew your food properly you don't need water to wash it down.

If you discover you enjoy colon cleansing, you may decide to do an herbal kidney cleanse once a year as well to keep these vital water-filtration organs in good shape.

THE LUNGS

Breathe deeply to allow your lungs to do their job of eliminating toxins. Most Westerners subventilate, taking in just enough air to sustain themselves. This is all tied in with feelings of low self-esteem: "I don't deserve," "I'm not good enough," and so on. If you are fearful, your shoulders will slouch forward as your body unconsciously tries to protect your heart region, and this will restrict your breathing still further.

Straighten your spine. Take heart. It is your birthright to live life to the full. With every breath you take, you are saying yes to life, yes to love, yes to joy, happiness, and abundance. Learn from the native peoples of the world or watch any newborn Western baby and discover that correct breathing is not shallow, involving only the upper chest, but deep from the diaphragm, allowing the internal organs to get massaged with every breath. Breathe through your nose, never through your mouth. Remember also to breathe when you eat, to oxygenate your food.

Other ways you can help your lungs are to take vigorous walks, avoid mucus-forming food that clogs them, avoid pollutants, and, of course, stop smoking if you're a smoker. If you need further incentive to quit, find a book or website that shows pictures of how grotesque the lungs of smokers are—it's quite a shock to see them.

THE LYMPHATIC SYSTEM

The lymphatic system cleanses all the tissues of the body. The blood has the heart to pump it around but the lymphatic system relies entirely on the action of the lungs and the muscles of the body, which is why regular exercise is so important. Walking, swimming, other forms of gentle exercise, and rebounding are excellent ways to get the lymph moving. Most types of massage are also helpful. So is dry skin brushing (see the next section about the skin).

One very important consideration is to avoid tight clothing, which will obstruct the flow of lymph in the body. In their book *Dressed to Kill*, Sydney Ross Singer and Soma Grismaijer warn of the health effects that can result from lymph restriction and toxic buildup caused by wearing bras, as well as "tight pants syndrome" in men.

From a survey of over 4,700 American women between 1991 and 1993 in their Bra and Breast Cancer study, they concluded that "the average American woman is 19 times more likely to develop breast cancer than is a woman who wears a bra for less than twelve hours daily" and "women who wear their bras all the time have a 113-fold increase in breast cancer when compared with women who wear their bras less than twelve hours daily." They note that in countries of the world where women have only recently begun wearing bras, breast cancer is just now becoming known. Puzzlingly, no one before or since has conducted a similar study, but in my opinion more research into this is long overdue.

Underwire bras, especially the sexy push-up variety, inhibit lymph drainage even more, and it is my belief that the metal also acts as a kind of antenna to conduct harmful electromagnetic fields from computers and other electrical appliances into the delicate breast tissue, contributing to the likelihood of breast cancer. Women working as computer operators, sewing machinists, and in other jobs where their breasts are in close proximity to the electromagnetic fields of electrical equipment are most at risk.

THE SKIN

Skin is amazing. Each square inch consists of about 19 million cells, 600 sweat glands, 90 oil glands, and 65 hairs; it is serviced by 19,000 nerve cells and 19 feet of intricately woven blood vessels, and populated by tens of millions of microscopic bacteria.

Functioning at capacity, our skin is designed to eliminate one third of the body's waste products, but in reality most people's skin functions poorly. Synthetic toiletries clog the pores and synthetic fabrics (latex, nylon, polyester, and so on) severely inhibit this natural process, particularly undergarments, because they are worn close to the skin. Far better to wear natural fabrics—pure cotton is the best, and linen, silk, and wool are also good—and avoid washing them with harsh biological liquids or powders, the residues of which are absorbed through your pores. Laundry balls and dryer balls are much more environmentally friendly alternatives to detergents and fabric softeners. They also cost far less in the long term, and don't infuse your fabrics with cheap artificial scents.

To help the skin, exercise, take saunas or Turkish baths to sweat out toxins, and do daily dry skin brushing to remove dead skin cells, clear out lymph, stimulate the glands, and prevent premature aging. This is best done in the morning before bathing. Always brush toward the heart and use a natural bristle brush. It feels fantastic!

21

Clearing Mental Clutter

If you have physical clutter in your home, you will also have clutter in your mind. Here's what to do about some of the most common forms of mental clutter.

STOP WORRYING

I once heard it said that worry is like a rocking horse—no matter how fast you go, you never move anywhere. Worry is in fact a complete waste of time and creates so much clutter in your mind that you cannot think clearly about anything.

The way to stop worrying is first of all to understand that you energize whatever you focus your attention on. Therefore, the more you allow yourself to worry, the more likely things are to go wrong. Worrying becomes such an ingrained habit that you have to consciously train yourself differently. Whenever you catch yourself fretting (and ask those close to you to point out when you're at it again), stop and change your thoughts. Focus your mind more productively on what you want to happen, rather than on what you are worried might happen, and dwell on what's already wonderful in your life, setting up a resonance for more wonderful stuff to come your way.

Make a list right now of all the things you worry about so that you'll spot them next time they turn up in your mind for a free rocking-horse session.

STOP CRITICIZING AND JUDGING

This is another total waste of time and energy, especially when you realize that everything you criticize and judge about others is something you don't like about yourself. The greatest criticizers are those who deep down believe, for whatever reason, that they themselves aren't good enough. Change these inner insecurities and the desire to demean others will magically melt away.

Another important thing to understand is that we humans see only a segment of reality in the greater cosmic scheme of things, so we are really never in a position to judge anyone or anything. A low-life street drunk may in essence be the kindest, sweetest soul you could ever meet, but if you judge him simply by appearances or get on some high moral platform about his behavior, you will miss that quality completely.

Don't clutter your mind with these pointless poison arrows. Instead, tune in to the highest aspects you can of everyone you meet and be amazed at how they in turn respond from the best of themselves.

STOP GOSSIPING

Stop constantly titillating yourself by gossiping about others. Gossip clutters your psyche and only shows how little of consequence is happening in your own life. Live and let live. Refuse to indulge in or listen to gossip or scandal in any form, and make it a point of integrity that you never say anything about anyone that you would not say to their face.

STOP MOANING AND COMPLAINING

Moaning, complaining, and blaming everything and everyone else for what is happening in your life clutters your speech and thoughts in such a way that most people don't even want to be around you. Focus on what you are grateful for and the gods will heap more goodies upon you. Keep moaning and groaning and you'll be on your own.

STOP MENTAL CHATTER

Psychologists estimate that the average person has about 60,000 thoughts per day. Unfortunately, 95 percent of those thoughts are exactly the same as the thoughts you had yesterday. And these are the same as the thoughts you had the day before that. And so on. In short, most of your mental process is unproductive, repetitive chatter going nowhere.

Another problem is the constant babble of external stimuli that is so prevalent in the Western lifestyle. Too many people have the TV or radio constantly turned on "for company," or spend their time reading trashy novels, aimlessly surfing the Net, and so on. Then suddenly one day, you are old or sick, and you realize you have done nothing with your life. All your thoughts are other people's thoughts, and you have no idea who you really are or what the purpose of your life might be.

When is the last time you had a genuinely new, completely original thought? The sad fact is that many people just continue day after day in the same old groove, filling their minds with the mundane clutter of day-to-day existence.

Make it a priority to have clarity in your life and fine-tune that clarity daily. Learn to meditate and experience the states of sublime stillness that it can bring. Quiet the chatter and open yourself to high spiritual connections that you can't possibly feel when you are a sea of noise and agitation.

TIE UP LOOSE ENDS

Get into the habit of tying up loose ends as soon as you become aware of them. For example, suppose you are talking with a friend who has a useful telephone number to give you. He or she knows the number, but offers to phone you with it tomorrow. It's astounding how often people put off until tomorrow what they can quite easily do today, and how much of an energy drain it is having to remember loose ends. Take the phone number then and there, and that is one less thing you have to do tomorrow.

Tie up other loose ends such as repaying any money you owe, returning any items you have borrowed, doing any errands you have said you would run, and anything else that is nagging away in the back of your mind to be done. Every unfulfilled promise or commitment has a call on your energy and pesters you to do it. If you know you can't keep your promise, it is far better to contact the person and let them know rather than just let the situation drift.

Here's an interesting thing I have learned from my own life experience, as a result of having dumped the word "should" from my vocabulary. Suppose I have promised to meet a friend on Thursday evening to go to a movie we both want to see. As Thursday approaches, I feel less and less inclined to go out that night. I can do one of two things: I can keep my promise and go because I said I would and therefore "should," or I can call my friend and cancel or postpone the date. I have found that on 90 percent of the occasions I have canceled or postponed, the other person was also wanting to do the same but had not wanted to let me down, so it worked out perfectly for both of us. The other 10 percent of the time people get a bit put out, but if they are honest with themselves, it is not usually me that has upset them. The problem is generally their inflexibility or the triggering of a memory of a much deeper upset from the past. See the next chapter for an understanding of upsets.

CLEAR YOUR COMMUNICATIONS

How many people do you have unresolved issues with? Think for a moment. Imagine yourself in a social setting. Who in your life, if they were to walk in the door, would immediately change your level of physical comfort? Who would make you feel that the room wasn't big enough for the two of you because of tensions between you? You may not consciously remember these people. In fact, you may actively try to keep them out of your thoughts. But your good old subconscious mind keeps track of them. Having unresolved communications in your life depletes your energy levels immensely.

If you sleep with someone, make especially certain that you keep your communications clear. Otherwise you will be fighting psychic battles with each other all night and will wake up feeling like you need a good night's sleep.

KEEP YOURSELF UP-TO-DATE

When everything is up-to-date in your life, you live in present time and can experience a feeling of surfing with the energy of life. Do whatever it takes to catch up with yourself and then keep it that way. You will have more energy than you ever believed possible. Children are like this. They live in the moment. And we all know how much vitality they have!

HANDLING INFORMATION OVERLOAD

How much information is there? The units of measurement themselves are awesome. We're not talking humble kilobytes (KB), significant megabytes (MB), or impressive gigabytes (GB)—one gigabyte being approximately the number of books full of information it would take to fill a pickup truck. We're not even talking terabytes (TB)—one terabyte being the equivalent of about 50,000 trees made into paper and printed. Or petabytes (PB)—200 petabytes representing approximately all the printed material on Earth. We've even exceeded exabytes (EB), which is 1,000 petabytes. Annual global Internet traffic is now measured in zettabytes (ZB), which is 1,000 exabytes. Beyond that is yottabytes (YB), and probably there will soon be a new unit called something like squiggabytes (SB?).

The point I am making here is that there is a *lot* of information in the world. It's on the same scale as what Douglas Adams says about space in his introduction to *The Hitchhiker's Guide to the Galaxy:* "Space is big. Really big. You just won't believe how vastly hugely mind-bogglingly big it is."

Neuroscientists have coined the term "infovore" to describe

the natural appetite humans have for new information. They have discovered the same pleasurable neural pathways are used when learning new facts as are activated by taking drugs such as heroin or morphine. In the same way that some people get addicted to Internet pornography, online social networking, gambling, or gaming, so do others get addicted to the "high" that comes from gathering information. Some infovores will spend hours and hours online searching for meaningful data, to the extent that it becomes a form of obsessive-compulsive behavior.

If this is part of your lifestyle, the question to ask yourself is, has this activity become a substitute for experiencing life firsthand? Are you living in a world of your own, with less and less real communication with people? And do you find that a large proportion of the material you are acquiring is not immediately useful but of the "just in case you need it" variety? If so, it is as much a form of clutter in your life as the physical kind that people keep for the same reason, and you need to engage in some form of therapy to discover the cause of your addiction and address it.

DECLUTTER YOUR MIND FOR RESTFUL SLEEP

If you lead a busy life and have lots of "things to do," you may find it difficult to switch off and relax. In particular, you may find your mind full of stuff when you want to go to sleep.

Here's a good tip: keep a notebook and pen by your bed and just before you go to sleep, scribble down all the things you have to remember to do. Then just forget about them and go to sleep. If you wake up in the night with more things on your mind, just open one eye, scribble them down, and go back to sleep. At first, you may need to keep a small flashlight next to your bed. With practice you can learn to write in the dark with your eyes shut. After a while you'll learn to get your whole list on paper in one go and sleep through the night, undisturbed by thoughts or worries.

The busier you are, the more important it is to completely relax and take time off to rest and regenerate at night. Learn to do the "night practice" technique described in Samuel Sagan's book, *Awakening the Third Eye*. This allows your higher subtle body complex to separate from your physical and etheric bodies, giving you the best night's sleep of all.

22

Clearing Emotional Clutter

Most people carry some form of emotional baggage. It prematurely ages us (I looked ten years younger after doing an intense year of personal work to clear out some of mine), and it gets in the way of everything we want to do.

UPSETS

If you're ever feeling upset about something, that's one of the best times to go and clear some clutter. Don't bother to pull yourself together before you begin. Just go to the cabinet with tears streaming down your face, bawling your head off if necessary, and pull everything out and begin sorting it. You'll be amazed how easy it is to sort clutter when you are in this condition. It almost seems to sort itself. You look at things you have been holding on to for years, and they seem so unimportant and obviously obsolete that there is no emotional tug at all as you sling them in the trash. You will also be amazed how sorting the clutter helps to calm you and gives you a new perspective on what was upsetting you. The act of letting go of the clutter also allows you to let go of your stuck feelings.

One teacher I studied with for a while used to say, if ever anyone was upset, "Will it matter ten years from now?" You get to see the issue from the viewpoint of your future self looking back with hindsight, and the answer is nearly always no.

You could say the same about most clutter. "Will I have found a use for this within the next ten years?" For most things you have been holding on to for a long time, the answer is nearly always no.

GRIEVANCES

One of the worst forms of emotional clutter is the type that results from grievances. Look deep within yourself to see who or what you need to forgive.

Sometimes people become so entrenched in their grievances that they refuse to even talk to each other. I have come across instances in families and married couples where these prolonged silences continue for days, weeks, months, years—even for decades. Some people actually go to their graves with these feelings stuck in their bodies, and it's a pretty sure bet that's what finished them off.

Sometimes these stuck feelings escalate to the level of disputes between whole families, groups, or nations, which create cancers in the emotional fabric of society. Attempts to resolve the situation by physical violence continue until one of the protagonists is brought to their knees, or a third and greater power steps in (called "diplomatic intervention") to bring them both to their senses. Diplomacy in this context can be defined as the art of harmonizing stuck emotional energy.

If you are the silent sulky type, understand that this may hurt the other person as you intend it to do, but it hurts you even more. Take a course in human relationships and learn a better way to handle your problems. Forgive and forget. Let go of your grievances and get on with your life.

CLEAR OUT YOUR FLAKY FRIENDS!

Do you know people who it always feels like an effort to talk to or who drain you when you are with them? Do you groan when you know so-and-so is calling you on the phone? I'm not talking here about good friends who are temporarily going through a rough patch or having a bad week. I am talking about negative people who are seriously past their "sell-by date," those you would like to be rid of but haven't had the guts or time to do anything about it.

One fascinating thing I've discovered is that just about everyone has a few of these unwanted "friends." I spent an entire dinner party once listening to the story of "the houseguest from hell" who turned up uninvited year after year and foisted herself on these people. For some inexplicable reason they never felt able to tell her how unwelcome she was, so year after year they endured her awful cooking and overbearing behavior, then complained about her ever after to everyone they knew.

Take a minute now to make a little list of people you'd really rather not know anymore. I'll pause the book while you do this . . .

Here's the interesting thing: if you have a list like this, and everyone else has a list like this, then—*whose list are you on?* Now there's some food for thought! Wouldn't it be best if we just got honest with one another about this and stopped these silly games?

There are billions of people in the world and you are free to choose whom to mix with. Choose kindred spirits who uplift and inspire you. The wonderful thing about having the courage to clear out all your moldy old friends is that it creates the space for you to attract wonderful, vital new relationships, providing you have made new decisions about what you will and will not have in your life. Eventually you will find that flaky people, energy vampires, and seriously negative individuals will not be in your life because your energy field feels too incompatible with theirs—they know that their chance of getting a free energy feed-up at your expense is nil, so they don't even bother trying.

MOVING ON FROM RELATIONSHIPS

Sometimes you realize it is not just an acquaintance who has become clutter in your life, but the person you thought was your significant other. Perhaps your lives have diverged and moved on to different paths, or maybe you never were compatible in the first place. The truth is that you have become clutter in each other's lives, although sometimes only one of you can see this at the time.

You now have two choices: do nothing, and wait for the relationship to crumble or explode apart on its own; or have the courage to act, to either repair the situation or leave it. If you still love, respect, and are good for each other, the chances are high that you can find a way for the relationship to continue, even though the form is sure to change in some way. Be sure to give it every chance of success. If it is time for you to move on, you will know in your heart that this is so.

In many instances it is, indeed, time to move on, and you do yourself and your partner a great disservice if you prolong the agony by delaying doing this too long. Scary as it may seem, if it is the right thing to do, you will discover that right alongside your quivering fear is another quivering energy called excitement. This is your

Higher Self thrilling at the prospect of the new opportunities that are about to open up in your life.

LETTING GO OF EMOTIONAL ARMOR

If your home is very cluttered you may feel the need to wear serious quantities of jewelry, probably to the extent that you may feel only half-dressed if you go out without it. Like house clutter, jewelry worn in this way is a form of emotional armor. After clearing your home, you will likely want to reduce the amount you wear because you feel more confident and able to let the natural "you" shine through.

23

Clearing Spiritual Clutter

Actually, this whole book has been about spiritual clutter. It's about the process of clearing away all the clutter that obscures our vision, confuses or misleads us, and hinders us on our path.

THIS SPECIAL TIME

We are fortunate to be alive in what the majority of spiritual teachers today believe is the most important time for human spiritual development in the history of our planet. It used to be that all the great knowledge of the world was held by just a few. Do you realize that nowadays you can attend a weekend workshop and learn the basics of what in centuries gone by would have taken years of dedicated apprenticeship to master? Not in the same depth, of course, but the fact is, these doors are now open and much of the knowledge and skills are available.

Holding on to things that keep us rooted in the past can therefore be totally counterproductive. When you think about how many times you are likely to have been reincarnated to be here today, surely your eternal Spirit is keen to be in present time, ready and able to go with what is happening now.

CALLING YOU BACK TO YOU

In Bali, they have a special ceremony known as "The Calling." It is understood that as a person goes through life, parts of themselves fracture and split off. If this happens too often or, in the case of a sudden, traumatic event, too quickly, it can weaken the Spirit of the person to a life-threatening extent. For example, after being injured in a road accident a vital part of the healing process is for the person to return with a priest to the place where it happened, to ceremonially purify the spot and call the part of their Spirit they left there back to themselves.

This ceremony is specific to Bali's form of Hindu religion and doesn't translate well to Western usage, but I mention it because a similar calling-back process happens when you clear the clutter in your life. As you release the things you no longer love or use, you call back to yourself the parts of your Spirit that have been attached to them, and attached to the emotional needs and memories associated with those objects. In so doing, you bring yourself powerfully into present time. Your energy, instead of being dispersed in a thousand different unproductive directions, becomes more centered and focused. You feel more spiritually complete and more at peace with yourself. All from simply clearing clutter. Amazing, isn't it?

LIVING CLUTTER-FREE

The higher purpose of clutter clearing is to help clear the debris that prevents us from connecting to the high spiritual realms we came from and to which we will return. It is all too easy to lose the plot down here, get immersed in materialism, and come to believe that this world is all there is, when in fact being here is only a short interlude in the spiritual journey each of us is on.

Clutter clearing in all its forms helps to restore clarity and simplicity. When you keep around you just the things you need for your personal journey instead of burdening yourself with things that obscure your way and hold you back, it is much easier to connect with your spiritual path. And when you have the sense of peace and purpose that comes with that, you will never feel the need for clutter again.

WHAT NEXT?

More Help

INSPIRING LETTERS

It's my sincere hope that reading this book will inspire and motivate you to clear clutter as never before, and many people have written to me over the years to tell me how much it has helped them. You can read a selection of these letters on my website (click on the Readers' Letters link in the Books section), which will hopefully inspire you to do likewise.

ONLINE COURSES

Feel that you need more help? I teach a range of online clutter clearing courses that you can take in the privacy of your own home, with ample time to put everything you learn into practice as you go along. As one participant said, "For me, this was a thousand times better than just reading a book."

My online courses have been taken by thousands of people from over fifty countries, and you can find full information about them on my website.

FIND A CLUTTER CLEARING PRACTITIONER

The good news is that it costs a heck of a lot less to hire a practitioner to help you let go of things than to acquire them in the first place, and it takes a lot less time, too.

On my website you can find an International Directory of Practitioners who have been personally trained by me to a very high level and also participate in continuing professional development programs each year to maintain and develop their knowledge and skills. If no one is listed in your part of the world, email info@karenkingston.com to ask if there are any practitioners willing to travel to where you live. This can often be arranged.

FREE MONTHLY NEWSLETTERS

Sign up on my website to receive free monthly newsletters containing news and articles about clutter clearing and related topics.

MY WEBSITE

I have a lively website that is regularly updated and contains a wealth of information that is not in my books.

website: www.karenkingston.com
email: info@karenkingston.com

Resources

PROFESSIONAL CLUTTER CLEARING PRACTITIONER TRAINING PROGRAM

My professional training covers a range of techniques and skills that are not taught in any other professional course. Major emphasis is placed on learning to discern the underlying reasons why a client has accumulated clutter in the first place, which allows them to gain a new perspective about it, and this in turn leads to a greater willingness to let it go. The training also includes advanced personal energy management techniques that I believe are essential for all professionals in this field of work to know and practice.

You can find more information at www.karenkingston.com

COLON-CLEANSING HERBS

Recommended supplier of Dr. Christopher's herbal colon-cleansing products:

Specialist Herbal Supplies
Portslade Hall, 18 Station Road, Portslade, BN41 1GB, UK
Tel: 0870 774 4494 (from abroad: +44 1273 424 333)

email: sales@shs100.com
website: www.shs100.com

High-quality herbs, sent with full information about how to do colon cleansing.

Reasonable prices, online ordering, and very quick international delivery service.

Also by Karen Kingston

Clear Your Clutter with Feng Shui (audiobook edition). For those who absorb information better by listening rather than reading, *Clear Your Clutter with Feng Shui* is available in CD audiobook format at karenkingston.com, and in digital audiobook format at Audible and Amazon.

Clear Your Clutter with Feng Shui (ebook edition). The ebook edition is widely available in all the most popular formats.

Creating Sacred Space with Feng Shui. Published by Piatkus, London, 1996, and Broadway Books, New York, 1997. This was my first book, designed as a companion volume to *Clear Your Clutter with Feng Shui*. However, there have been so many new developments in the field of space clearing since it was written that parts of it are now very out of date. Visit www .karenkingston.com for information about my latest book on this subject.

Bibliography and Recommended Reading

COLON CLEANSING AND BETTER HEALTH

Anderson, Richard. *Cleanse and Purify Thyself* (Christobe Publishing, 2007)

Dufty, William. *Sugar Blues* (Grand Central Life & Style, 1986)

Gray, Robert. *The Colon Health Handbook: New Health Through Colon Rejuvenation* (Emerald Publishing, 1990)

Jensen, Bernard. *Dr. Jensen's Guide to Better Bowel Care: A Complete Program for Tissue Cleansing Through Bowel Management* (Avery Publishing Group, 1998)

Singer, Sydney Ross, and Soma Grismaijer. *Dressed to Kill: The Link Between Breast Cancer and Bras* (Avery Publishing Group, 1995)

HEALING AND METAPHYSICS

Diamond, John. *Life Energy: Using the Meridians to Unlock the Hidden Power of Your Emotions* (Paragon House, 1990)

Hay, Louise. *Heal Your Body* (Hay House, 1984)

OBSESSIVE-COMPULSIVE DISORDERS

Dumont, Raeann. *The Sky Is Falling: Understanding and Coping with Phobias, Panic, and Obsessive-Compulsive Disorders* (W. W. Norton & Company, 1997); see chapter 12: Mr. More, The Man Who Couldn't Throw Anything Away

PHILOSOPHY

Bloom, Howard. *The Lucifer Principle* (Atlantic Monthly Press, 1995)
Hoff, Benjamin. *The Tao of Pooh* (Penguin, 1983)

PROCRASTINATION

Tracy, Brian. *Eat That Frog!: 21 Great Ways to Stop Procrastinating and Get More Done in Less Time* (Berrett-Koehler Publishers, 2006). Also available as an ebook at www.briantracy.com

REFERENCES

Emmons, Robert A. and McCullough, Michael E. *Counting Blessings Versus Burdens: An Experimental Investigation of Gratitude and Subjective Well-being in Daily Life* (*Journal of Personality and Social Psychology,* 2003, Vol. 84, No. 2, 377–89)

Lefcourt, Herbert M. *Locus of Control: Current Trends in Theory and Research* (2nd ed. Hillsdale, N.J.: Lawrence Erlbaum Associates, 1982)

Mark, Gloria and Picard, Rosalind. *How interruptions can destroy your day* (article by Alison Motluk, *New Scientist,* Issue 2557, June 21, 2006)

SPIRITUAL KNOWLEDGE

Sagan, Dr. Samuel. *Awakening the Third Eye* (Clairvision School Foundation, 1997)

Sagan, Dr. Samuel. *Knowledge Track: Death, the Great Journey* (Clairvision School, 2001). Can be purchased online at www.clairvision.org.

QUOTATIONS

Adams, Douglas. *The Hitchhiker's Guide to the Galaxy* (Del Rey, 1995)

Adler, Bill. *The Uncommon Wisdom of Oprah Winfrey: A Portrait in Her Own Words* (Aurum Press, 1997)

Godin, Seth. "Don't Shave That Yak!" (Seth's Main Blog, March 5, 2005), http://sethgodin.typepad.com/seths_blog/2005/03/dont_shave_that.html

Index